"This book holds ancient truths for [...] attention. Truths about forgiveness [...] of the gospel message many of us [...] has been harmed—which is all of [...] like way despite his or her wound... ... ... [...] free and is bold enough to acknowledge freedom can't exist without forgiveness."

—**Pricelis Dominguez**, author of *Being a Sanctuary*, pastor, and founder of Full Collective

"If you're looking for clarity on forgiveness, including its scope and the distinctions between sinful offenses and personal preferences while learning to navigate relationship challenges with love and resilience, then *Living Beyond Offense* is the perfect resource for you. Yana engages her audience with wisdom, grace, competence, and compassion. *Living Beyond Offense* is ideal for anyone struggling with forgiveness while striving to obey God's command to love Him and others as oneself."

—**Leonard Omar King**, MDiv, EdD candidate, Bridgehaven Counseling Associates, staff counselor

"Unforgiveness is a silent and deadly cancer lurking in the hearts of many people both inside and outside the church. In this practical and theologically rich work, Yana Conner shows us how to pull bitterness up by its roots. Forgiveness is at the very center of Christianity. But, ironically, very few of us can articulate what it is—or how to actually forgive. This book grounds our forgiveness in the grace of Jesus and gives an incredibly practical roadmap for this difficult but life-giving journey."

—**J.D. Greear**, pastor, the Summit Church; author, *Gospel: Recovering the Power That Made Christianity Revolutionary*

"Yana Conner has blessed us with so much more than familiar language on forgiveness. Instead, she's given us a roadmap, a travel companion in herself, and sweet hope wrapped in the light of the gospel to help us see a beautiful life beyond offense. If you've tried to forgive but still feel stuck by offense, I implore you to read *Living Beyond Offense*. Yana's writing is approachable, empathic, and laced with what we need most—the words of Scripture to reorient us to Jesus's kingdom culture and the way of shalom."

—**Dr. Sarita T. Lyons**, preacher, Bible teacher, church leader, psychotherapist, and author of *Church Girl: A Gospel Vision to Encourage* and *Challenge Black Christian Women.*

"*Living Beyond Offense* is a theologically rich and compassionate call to the costly, freeing path of forgiveness. Yana Jenay Conner speaks with clarity and courage into the real tensions of abuse, boundaries, and obedience. This book is a needed guide for anyone serious about following Jesus."

—**Brenna Blain**, contemporary theologian and bestselling author

"Yana's words in *Living Beyond Offense* are timely and transformational. Not many books can bring me to tears, challenge and convict me, and leave me feeling hopeful all at the same time, but this book has done it. Her explanation of what it means to 'turn the other cheek' and how to forgive when you can't forget will sit with me for a long time. *Living Beyond Offense* is a masterful work that is theologically robust yet also practical. This book is one of the best teachings I have ever heard on forgiveness and is a must read."

—**Lisa Fields**, author of *When Faith Disappoints* and
CEO and founder of the Jude 3 Project

"Yana goes straight to the heart of one of the core causes of ruptured relationships: offense. She approaches the topic with a rare blend of biblical depth, compassionate challenge, and tender kindness. She doesn't shy away from the truth or from the gentle care so many of us need as we navigate the painful realities of deep relationships. This book is an essential guide for anyone longing to build healthy relationships with others without sacrificing their own well-being. Yana asks and answers the questions we all wrestle with as we navigate hardship in relationships. *Living Beyond Offense* offers both wisdom and warmth to those committed to healing and cultivating meaningful connection within community. Many will be blessed by this powerful and timely work."

—**Kobe Campbell**, trauma therapist, author, and speaker

"What Yana Conner has accomplished with her work in *Living Beyond Offense* is nothing short of brilliant, timely, and refreshing. Yana captures both the heart and the hope of biblical forgiveness. This book offers a comprehensive understanding of the truth of forgiveness while navigating the challenges we all have with forgiveness. While Yana's authentic transparency makes the book accessible, her biblical clarity makes the subject of forgiveness approachable. Healing, hope, and help are found in every chapter!"

—**Ryan Brooks**, lead pastor, Vertical Church; author of *I Am Called: Answering the Call of God with a Life on Mission*

LIVING BEYOND OFFENSE

YANA JENAY CONNER

HARVEST HOUSE PUBLISHERS
EUGENE, OREGON

Published in association with the literary agency of Wolgemuth & Wilson.

Cover design and illustration by Bryce Williamson
Interior design by KUHN Design Group

For bulk, special sales, or ministry purchases, please call 1-800-547-8979.
Email: CustomerService@hhpbooks.com

This logo is a federally registered trademark of the Hawkins Children's LLC. Harvest House Publishers, Inc., is the exclusive licensee of this trademark.

To Ma

*None of this is possible apart from
your unwavering love.*

CONTENTS

PART 5: TRUSTING AGAIN...173

FOREWORD

Early in my career, I found myself caught in the middle of a conflict, unfairly cast as the scapegoat for a situation I hadn't caused. To make matters worse, several of my coworkers chose to believe the false information being spread about me and responded by giving me the silent treatment for months. To say that their response took a toll on me mentally and emotionally would be an understatement. The silence was devastating, leaving me with a thin slice of hope that things would turn around.

But one day, they did.

While standing in line for a staff training, I found myself right behind one of the coworkers who had distanced themselves from me. Upon seeing me, she smiled and suddenly began to make small talk. At first I was perplexed, wondering why she had decided to start talking to me again. However, my curiosity quickly wore off, and anger took its place. Her mistreatment of me had caused me so much internal damage, and her newfound "friendliness" failed to acknowledge it. She wanted to jump back into our relationship as though nothing had happened, and I was not about to let that slide.

That's when I heard the Lord impress upon my heart two simple words: *Forgive her.*

He quickly reminded me that He loved her as much as He loved me and that I needed to reflect His love by walking in forgiveness. At that moment, I was being driven by my woundedness and desire for vengeance. God's words stopped me right in my tracks and reminded me of a truth I could not get past: Since God had forgiven me, I had to extend that same forgiveness to anyone who wronged me. No exceptions or exempt clauses would let me hide from my responsibility to forgive.

If I'm honest, I don't think I'm the only one who has tried to hide from their forgiveness responsibilities. You probably have too; that's part of the reason you picked up this book. Forgiveness is one of the spiritual disciplines we'd like to skip over. We easily find rationalizations for why our specific situation is exempt from Jesus's command to forgive (Matthew 6:14-15). We've become skilled at living in the gray area of forgiveness, treating it like an ideal that is only achievable for super spiritual Christians.

Often this is because the call to forgive comes when we are still in pain. Taking this step of obedience while we are carrying deep anger or trying to heal from the wounds inflicted by someone else's sinful actions is incredibly difficult. It is hard to release our grip on what we are owed, trusting that God will make all things right. This kind of release doesn't come naturally; it must be learned. And even then, forgiveness is not a onetime choice, but one we must make repeatedly.

This book will help you learn how to do this, and your guide is well acquainted with the difficulty of the task. Yana is one of my dearest friends, and I have seen her wrestle with the truth she has included in these pages. Her faith is both contemplative and courageous. She doesn't settle for easy answers, but instead does the hard work that has produced a spiritual tree whose roots run deep and wide (Jeremiah 17:7-8).

What you will find in this book is the fruit of her labor: wisdom that is coated in vulnerability, conviction, and compassion. Instead of giving you a shallow how-to guide, Yana invites you to explore the true meaning of forgiveness, why it matters, and how it leads to flourishing not only for others but also for yourself.

To do this, she draws on a rich theology of shalom—the beautiful wholeness we were created to experience and the one Christ invites us to cultivate as we wait for Him to restore it in full. Yana and I have spent countless conversations basking in the beauty of shalom. We have wrestled with our imperfect experience of it, rejoiced when God has used us to help share it with someone else, and seen our faith be held together by shalom when the storms of life tried to knock us down.

Since she is a talented writer, Yana makes her theological reflection practical by graciously sharing her own stories. Sprinkled throughout the book are snippets from her life that are encouraging, challenging, and at times heartbreaking. Her sacrifice of honesty proves she has lived out the wisdom principles she will share with you. Her experience also allows her to shine a light into the corners where we try to hide from our forgiveness responsibilities. She knows all the excuses and "get out of forgiveness" passes we try to give ourselves. She pulls them into the light of the gospel for God to heal and restore.

Friend, you picked up this book to learn how to forgive, but you will leave with so much more. You are about to embark on a life-changing journey. It won't be easy, but it will be more than worth it because forgiveness isn't just a choice we make to free ourselves; it's a choice we make to live in the way of the Kingdom of God, bearing witness to our glorious King as we eagerly wait for Him to return.

—Elizabeth Woodson

INTRODUCTION

My father was my first teacher in forgiveness. His frequent absence, sporadic contributions to assist my mom with my care, and unfair ability to win you over with a smile even though you knew he would hurt you again made him the primary vehicle God would use to teach me my very first lessons on forgiveness. When my dad entered a room, I lit up. When he didn't, I painfully longed for his presence. I was a daddy's girl without a dad. I spent countless days standing behind the screen door, waiting for him to make good on his promise to come. Though I had the unwavering love and sufficient care of my mother and grandmother, I spent most of my childhood trying to answer this nagging question: *Why isn't my dad here?*

The answers were in the tingly smell that often came with his hugs and the slur of his tongue on the rare occasion he called. But as a kid, you don't know the signs of alcoholism; you don't even know the word for it. All you know is the pain that's there when your father isn't. With no definitive answer, I subscribed to the "It Is What It Is" method for coping with my pain. Fatherlessness was common among my family members and friends. Who was I to sulk over my daddy wounds? However, as you can imagine, this coping method only worked for so long.

In 2008, while interning with a campus ministry right out of college, I was asked to give a presentation on the felt needs of Black college students. During my preparation, I came across this statistic: 73

percent of African American children are born into a single-parent home.[1] My usual response to this kind of information was to shrug my shoulders with indifference. But on this day, I cried. First, for the 73 percent. Then, for me. For the first time, I allowed myself to feel the pain. To fully feel the ache of my dad's absence and honestly acknowledge its impact on my life. As I cried, God's presence tangibly moved in on me, helping me to see that just because something's common doesn't mean it doesn't hurt. My father's absence hurt, and it should.

I often jokingly refer to the days and years following this tender moment with God as the "Dark Ages." Though honestly acknowledging my pain was a necessary step for the journey of forgiveness ahead, it unleashed the anger I had suppressed for years. That following Sunday, I went to church, sat in the back, and impatiently waited for the pastor to invite people down for prayer. My newfound anger left me feeling fragile, on edge, and unsure of how to move forward. I wanted relief. But I would quickly learn that forgiveness and healing don't magically appear at the end of every *amen*.

Understanding what I did not, the elder who prayed for me suggested I consider counseling to address my daddy wounds. After three sessions, I felt worse, not better, and quit. The counselor asked me questions I wasn't ready to answer and uncovered emotions I wasn't ready to explore. Those unanswered questions and suppressed feelings were maintaining my fragile sense of safety. Would I be able to recover if I honestly went *there*? I wasn't ready to take the risk. I wasn't ready to get that close to the pain. However, this also meant I wasn't anywhere close to being ready to forgive.

While I couldn't really do much about not being ready to dive headfirst into the pain and the work of forgiveness, this came at a cost. My family members and close friends often found themselves on the other side of my anger and pain. They paid for the failings of my father *and* my inability to forgive. But, unlike my father, they didn't abandon me. They didn't leave. They stayed. And I can honestly say it was their trustworthy love, gentle questioning, and gracious correction that prepared my heart to forgive my dad 11 years later.

At times I feel a deep sense of shame that it took that long for me to forgive. I mean, wasn't I a Christian? Didn't the Spirit of the living God reside within me? Why couldn't I just forgive? Though there were seasons within that 11-year span where I made a concerted effort to forgive my dad with holiday phone calls, Father's Day cards, and attempts to get breakfast when I was in town, forgiveness seemed elusive. It was hard to move past the memories of drunken phone calls, traumatic weekend visits, and eagerly waiting to be picked up only to be forgotten. It was also hard because nothing was changing. Not dad or my feelings. Forgiveness felt impossible.

Paul, in Philippians 3:15-16, provides a helpful explanation for my 11-year struggle. After sharing his resolve to forget what lies behind and press toward the prize before him, he writes:

> Let those of us who are mature think this way, and if in anything you think otherwise, God will reveal that also to you. *Only let us hold true to what we have attained* (emphasis mine).

Yes, I was a Christian, and the Spirit of God lived within me. But at this point in my walk with Christ, I was still very much a spiritual toddler. I could only hold true—live up—to what I had attained. And what I had attained up until this point in my walk with God was a fuzzy understanding of Jesus's command to forgive. I knew I was called to do it, but I didn't entirely understand why or know how.

It's possible you've picked up this book because even though you know Jesus calls His followers to forgive, you don't fully understand why or how either. You read verses about turning the other cheek and loving your enemies (Matthew 5:39, 44), and you say to yourself or

God, "Why?" Or maybe you've been a Christian for a while, have heard some good sermons on these topics, and walk out of church inspired to forgive, but are not sure how to go about it. You've tried forgetting, ignoring, or forcing your feelings to change, but nothing works. If this is your struggle, this book has been written with you in mind. My fervent prayer is that with each page turn, you will gain more clarity on why Jesus calls you to forgive and how to do it. My hope is that with each chapter, you will encounter the *compelling whys* and *practical hows* you need to do the hard work of forgiveness God's way.

However, I didn't write this book as an expert on forgiveness. I can honestly say I have not excelled spiritually in this area and almost didn't write this book because of it. Consider me less of an expert and more of a fellow weary traveler, wandering alongside you in the wilderness of suffering and trying to live out her faith. In so many of these chapters, I am working out my theology, wrestling with my feelings, and seeking to live in response to Jesus's command to forgive. As you read this book, I invite you to do the same. When you encounter Jesus's teaching on how we are called to live in His world, consider what you believe and why you believe it. As I share my own stories of forgiveness and those of others, let them lead you to reflect on your own. And as I attempt to put language to what God taught me through His Word about the hard work of forgiveness, join me in seeking to respond in faith and obedience. However, do so at a pace that allows you to hold true—live up—to the truth you attain as you read this book.

Walking through the pain of offense and engaging in the work of forgiveness can be emotionally taxing. You will need to pace yourself. If you get to the end of a section within a chapter and need to take a break, take it. Though I believe there is a true finish line to the work of forgiveness, you're in a marathon, not a sprint. You may need to take this book slow to work out your theology—your view of God, self, and how God created the world to work—and make space to wrestle with your past hurts. To help you do this, at the end of each chapter, you will be invited to selah—to pause and think about what you just read and sit with whatever God might be bringing to the surface. Often our lives are moving fast and we either don't *have* or don't *make* the time to process them. But if you are going to live beyond offense, you will need to slow down to talk to God and allow God to talk to you. As my good sis Pricelis Dominguez, a champion of the selah practice, explains, you will need to "live slower...process Scripture slower, and become more introspective *in light of the presence of God.*"[2] You may be tempted to skip these parts, but I encourage you not to. Make time to sit in the light of God's presence long enough for Him to heal the place within you that feels broken. Give your soul the space to feel what it feels. And as you do, may God be ever so gracious to you, revealing to you the truths you need to forgive and live beyond offense.

PART 1

WE LIVE IN A STORY

You and I live in a story much grander than our own. The rising and falling action of our individual narratives is all swept up in the metanarrative found in our Bibles. This metanarrative progresses in four overarching movements—God's creation, humanity's fall, Christ's rescue, and humanity's resurrection. Each movement not only reveals to us the glory of the gospel story, but also provides us with the source material we need to make sense of life.

In the opening pages of our Bibles, we find the good intentions of God's heart and the life we're all longing for. *God creates* a world absent of imperfections. A world filled with harmony and unbridled love. However, things quickly take a bad turn. *Humanity falls* away from God's law. Sin enters God's good and perfect world, bringing death, conflict, and suffering along with it. This part of the story creates a new reality: one we weren't made for and desperately want to escape.

Though humanity falls away from God, He doesn't fall away from them. Instead, He doubles down on His love and sends His Son,

Jesus. Here, the metanarrative reaches its climax. Jesus enters the story answering the questions: Is there a better way to live? Does God care? And is there any hope? His answer to all of them is a resounding yes! Through His sinless life, Jesus gives us a renewed vision for how to live in relationship with God and others. Through His death, *Christ rescues* all who would believe in Him from the pending debt of their sins, revealing the eternal depths of God's care for us. Through His resurrection, He secures the coming of *humanity's resurrection*, giving them a hope and a future they don't deserve.

Beloved, if you are a Christian, this is your story. This is your song. In the final pages of our Bibles, we are told that all who tether their narratives to this metanarrative will share its end. Sin, death, conflict, and suffering will not be the end of their story; glory will. The beginning of God's story will be restored, and they will enjoy eternity with Christ in a new creation absent of imperfection.

In this section, we are going to explore this story to make sense of why our human relationships are often less than ideal and discover who Christ calls us to be as we wait for our resurrection. We are going to talk about, as Charaia Rush puts it in her book *Courageously Soft*, the "tension that exists as our beings tread this space between the garden and glory."[1] Much of living beyond offense is predicated on how we believe we are meant to live in this tension. And the question hanging over this tension and the entirety of this book is this: Will you allow the story God is telling to shape the way you live, or will you choose another story?

CHAPTER 1

A TRUTH WE MUST ACCEPT

No one is good except God alone.

JESUS, LUKE 18:19

We live in a broken world with fallen people. *People will fail us. We will fail people.* People will, knowingly or unknowingly, fall short of meeting our very reasonable expectations. Even the ones who love us dearly will inevitably hurt our feelings and sin against us. And we, them. There are even times when we deeply harm one another, leaving each other with scars that make it difficult to move in the world without an intrusive amount of anger, anxiety, and shame. We live in a broken world with fallen people. This is where we are in the biblical story that is unfolding, and this is the biblical truth we must accept. However, when our lives collide with this truth, it hurts and is a painful reminder that this isn't the world our good and perfect God created us for.

WE WERE CREATED FOR SHALOM

In Genesis 1–2, we find Adam and Eve standing face-to-face, naked and unashamed. Though naked literally means to be "unclothed," Adam and Eve's nakedness surpassed what could be physically seen. Both their inner and outer person laid bare before the other. With no feelings of shame, neither felt the need to hide from one another or God. Free of insecurities, neither was so preoccupied with how their hair looked that they couldn't be enamored of the beauty of the other. They weren't sizing each other up in comparison or competition, for they understood that in God's good and perfect creation, there was enough space for them both. In God's lush garden, Adam and Eve felt and were truly safe with one another. Hurt and harm weren't conceivable or possible. For they lived in a reality filled with uninterrupted shalom.

In our English Bibles, the Hebrew word *shalom* is often translated as "peace." In our modern context, peace is primarily understood as a sense of tranquility. However, in Hebrew, the original language of the Old Testament, the definition of shalom encompasses much more. Shalom is a state of complete and utter wholeness. It's a reality where everyone has what they need to survive and thrive. Nothing is broken or in danger of harm. Where shalom exists, bodies are well, and relationships are whole. Peace—feelings of tranquility and quiet—flow because in the presence of shalom, the fear of death is unfounded, the temptation to sin is nonexistent, and relational and societal conflict is unimaginable. Shalom is a world completely at rest, absent of any tear, crack, or break. In such a place, humans are free to run wholeheartedly naked without shame.

A PEOPLE MARKED BY SELF-CONSCIOUS, SELF-CENTERED SELF-PRESERVATION

We know nothing of this naked and unashamed bliss. Instead of enjoying relationships filled with shalom, we wearifully tarry with ones marked by some measure of *self-conscious, self-centered self-preservation*. The very moment Adam and Eve sinned against God, the shalom they once enjoyed began to unravel. Immediately they became aware of their nakedness and became shamefully *self-conscious*. They stitched fig leaves together to conceal parts of themselves that once thrived unhidden. Their human need for acceptance was introduced to the fear of rejection, and now they felt a strong need to protect their hearts. As overly self-conscious beings, they also became painfully *self-centered.* Their ability to love one another freely was now constrained by consuming thoughts of self. Their commitment to having one another's back became complicated by the deep sense of needing to look out for their own, which is exactly what Adam did next in the Genesis story.

When God approached Adam to get clarity as to why they collectively rejected His command, Adam shifted the blame. The woman he once sang over as his greatest complement, he now claimed was his greatest liability. When asked by God, "Did you eat from the tree that I commanded you not to eat from?" (Genesis 3:11 CSB), Adam replied, "The woman you gave to be with me—she gave me some fruit from the tree, and I ate" (Genesis 3:12 CSB). My good friend Josh Reed calls this a classic case of *self-preservation.* Adam, taking no responsibility for his actions or inaction, threw the "bone of [his] bones" under the bus in a faulty attempt to preserve his right standing before God (Genesis 2:23). He tried to absolve himself of any responsibility and shame by shaming and blaming his wife, making her solely responsible for their shared sin. What began as a fracture in their relationship with stitched fig leaves was now utterly broken with Adam's *self-conscious, self-centered, self-preserving* betrayal.

From Genesis 3 onward, we encounter story after story of human relationships marked by *self-conscious, self-centered self-preservation.* Cain, Adam's son, out of competition and comparison, killed his brother, Abel, to cover his *self-conscious* insecurities (Genesis 4). Shechem, without care or consent, took the body of Jacob's daughter, Dinah, to satisfy *his own* sexual desires. In bringing pleasure to his body, he traumatized Dinah's whole personhood—physically, emotionally, and socially (Genesis 34). Pharoah's hard, *self-conscious, self-centered,* and *self-preserving* heart led him to seek the genocide of an entire nation (Exodus 1). King David, after taking Bathsheba's body without her permission, killed her husband to preserve his reputation (2 Samuel 11). The people of Israel, looking out for their own interest, failed to obey God's commands to care for the poor, welcome the foreigner, and love their neighbor as they loved themselves.

Jesus entered the story and ushered in a new Kingdom, but the stories of *self-conscious, self-centered self-preservation* continued. Though Jesus willingly went to Calvary, the Pharisees' self-conscious envy, Judas's self-centered greed, Pilate's self-preserving cowardness, and an angry crowd's rejection paved the way. Though His sacrificial death and powerful resurrection provided a way for shalom to be restored between us, God, and one another, what we found after Jesus's ascension to heaven wasn't a quick fix. Even Paul, who wrote the majority of the New Testament, found himself contending with the reality of living in a broken world with fallen people. God had set him and Barnabas apart during a prayer gathering to preach the gospel to the Gentiles, but after a "sharp disagreement," their relational shalom unraveled (Acts 15:36-41). Even Paul and Barnabas, who were filled with the Spirit and fruitful in ministry, were unable to escape their broken reality. And, for now, neither can we.

Over the past 21 centuries, we've added countless stories of self-conscious, self-centered self-preservation to the human record. Being overly self-conscious, we attempt to conceal our true selves with lies. Living in a world structured by the "isms" of race, sex, and class, self-preservation is a way of life. To preserve our egos or sense of safety, to protect ourselves, or to ensure the people who've sinned against us experience the same amount of pain they've caused, we use words with sharp edges. We no longer innately enjoy one another uninterrupted. Instead, we get annoyed, fight, bicker, belittle, use, and abuse one another for personal gain—even if that personal gain is as petty as getting the last word in an argument. As a result, we become both victims and perpetrators of acts of self-conscious, self-centered self-preservation.

THE TRUTH WE MUST ACCEPT

Beloved, you live in a broken world with broken people, and because this is your reality, you need to abandon the expectation for our relationships to be absent of imperfections, struggles, or offense. However, the invitation to accept this truth isn't meant to lead you into isolation. I get the strategy. I've tried it. It doesn't work. Isolation depresses the soul. You and I were created for relationships. We were created in the image of a relational God and are inherently relational. Yes, people can make you angry, but they can also fill your life with joy. Yes, they possess the ability to hurt you. But they are also often the very ones you need to heal. At their best, they are compassionate, trustworthy, and a lot of fun. If you distance yourselves from others in fear of experiencing pain, you won't let people get close enough for you to experience the gift of being loved. Choosing isolation or keeping people around but passively at bay is not how we should respond to this truth. Here are two sober ways we should respond.

1. Don't be shocked.

No one is good but God (Mark 10:18). In this broken world with fallen people, people will hurt and even fail us. Offense will happen. It's inevitable. Though we should not live in fear of getting hurt, we do need to live in awareness that it will happen. While being shocked is a warranted response to offense, especially in our closest relationships, this awareness helps us not be so shocked that we are unable or unwilling to do the hard work of forgiveness. It also helps us create enough space in our relationships for people to be less than perfect. Not harmful, but imperfect.

2. Be Prepared to do the work of forgiveness.

Trauma therapist Kobe Campbell writes,

> Every meaningful, intimate, and trusting relationship will
> experience what is known as a rupture…it's an unavoidable
> part of every relationship. No matter how much love, care,
> or intention we bring, we will, at some point, hurt or be
> hurt by those we are in a relationship with. The strength
> of a relationship is not determined by the absence of
> rupture but by the presence of repair.[1]

If we want "meaningful, intimate, and trusting" relationships, we must prepare our hearts for the days we will need to repair the ruptures that naturally occur. If we want our relationships to live beyond offense, we will need to learn how to thoughtfully address conflict, communicating our hurts, asking curious questions, and being eager to restore relational shalom. If we want long-lasting relationships, we must learn how to forgive. In this broken and fallen world, forgiveness is a necessary survival skill.

THE STARTING POINT

After a stint of going missing, my dad called. Since I was in a season of making a concerted effort to forgive, I answered. Immediately, I regretted it. My dad was drunk and within minutes said something hurtful. I wanted to hang up on him, but with the Spirit's help, I hurried him off the phone instead. While trying to bring my heart rate down before I transitioned to the next thing, I started to plot my relational exit strategy. No more phone calls. No more attempts to see him when I was in town. But before I could get too far along in my planning, God's presence tangibly moved in on me as it did before. However, this time, it wasn't an invitation to give me more space to express my feelings. It was an invitation to extend more grace.

My dad was a fallen human being. Alcoholism had stifled his ability to be the kind of dad he had proven he could be when he was sober. He also was a fallen human being who had yet to experience the life change that comes through faith in Jesus. The Spirit of God did not reside within him, empowering him to resist the urge to drink or compelling him to bridle his tongue. Though his actions were harmful and wrong, and I didn't need to abandon my desires for a sober father, I was holding him to a standard he was ill-equipped to meet. I needed to adjust my expectations and create more space for him to be a fallen and yet-to-be-redeemed human.

While I still had a long way to go in my journey of forgiving my father, accepting the truth that my dad was a fallen human being was the starting point. For the first time, my anger was joined by compassion. From that moment forward, I let go of my expectations of having a perfect father and embraced the one I had—and that the one I had needed forgiving.

SELAH: At the end of each chapter, you will have an opportunity to *selah*—pause and think—about your own story and how it interacts with the truths shared. My prayer is that with each selah you would encounter God through His Word, better understand your pain, and find your way closer to forgiving those who've offended you. To help with this, each selah will be framed by *Lectio Divina*, the ancient meditative practice. This practice of reading and rereading God's Word helps move the truths of Scripture from your head to your heart, fueling fruitful and faith-filled obedience. During this practice, you will *read* a passage of Scripture, *reflect* on your story, *respond* to the Word's truths, and *rest* in God's promises. For our first selah, we'll spend time mediating on Psalm 103:8-14:

8 The LORD is merciful and gracious,
slow to anger and abounding in steadfast love.
9 He will not always chide,
nor will he keep his anger forever.
10 He does not deal with us according to our sins,
nor repay us according to our iniquities.
11 For as high as the heavens are above the earth,
so great is his steadfast love toward those who fear him;
12 as far as the east is from the west,
so far does he remove our transgressions from us.
13 As a father shows compassion to his children,
so the LORD shows compassion to those who fear him.
14 *For he knows our frame;*
he remembers that we are dust (emphasis mine).

READ: Read Psalm 103:8-14 slowly and pause over any words or phrases that stand out to you.

REFLECT: Read Psalm 103:8-14 slowly and pause over the last verse. Consider the evidence in your life that testifies to the truth that God has remembered you are dust and has been compassionate toward you.

RESPOND: Read Psalm 103:13-14 slowly. Consider what faulty expectations you have put on your relationships and those who are made of dust.

- What faulty expectations of your relationships do you need to abandon to accept the truth that you live in a broken world with fallen people?

- Who are you holding to standards they are likely ill-equipped to meet because of their dusty frame?

REST: Celebrate and rest in the truth that God is merciful, compassionate, slow to anger, and abounding in steadfast love. Allow yourself to be swept up in the picture of Him as your compassionate Father, remembering that you are only dust.

CHAPTER 2

BLESSED ARE THE SHALOM-MAKERS

Blessed are the peacemakers,
for they will be called children of God.

JESUS, MATTHEW 5:9 NIV

There I was, sitting in a room filled with people I admired and loved, ready to walk out. For the past hour we had gone back and forth about what was and was not said and what should and should not be done, with little to no forward progress. I was exhausted. I had been in several meetings like this since May 2020 and was starting to wonder if the whole multiethnic church idea was worth it. I was tired of explaining, weary of listening, and emotionally drained by everything that was happening inside and outside that room. The growing death toll due to COVID-19, police brutality against people of color, and hate crimes against Asian Americans and Pacific Islanders were weighing heavily on my soul. The racial and political tensions flooding my social media feed and close relationships left me wanting to create distance socially and emotionally. Though I had long been captivated by the apostle John's revelation of every nation, tribe, and tongue worshipping around God's throne, I started to question if it was possible to experience a meaningful measure of it on this side of heaven. And even if so, was it worth it?

Sitting across the room from me, another leader was reaching their own point of exhaustion. With tears in their eyes, they began to share how painful it was to have those they regarded as family believe the worst of them. Though their assessment was warranted, I found their tearful vulnerability annoying. *How dare they cry? How dare they ask for understanding and compassion? I'm the minority! My tears have been unending for months!* Before I could fix my lips to say those words out loud, the Spirit invited me to choose another way—to choose the path of shalom.

BLESSED ARE THE SHALOM-MAKERS

In His inaugural sermon on the Kingdom of heaven, Jesus presents eight groups of people He considers blessed. Among them are the peacemakers. He says, "Blessed are the peacemakers, for they will be called children of God" (Matthew 5:9 NIV). Of all the other groups, Jesus reserves the title of God's child for those who "work for peace"— shalom (NLT). In referring to them this way, it's as if Jesus is saying that those who make shalom bear witness to the very DNA of God living within them. As shalom-makers, they are the spitting image of the Father, the Master Shalom-Maker, who through the person of Jesus Christ brings shalom to all things, everywhere. No one could deny that a shalom-maker belongs to Him. When they are engaged in the work of shalom, they bear God's image so winsomely, proving that He is their Father, and they are His child.

Later in this sermon, Jesus gives the same commendation to another group: those who love their enemies. In Matthew 5:43-45, Jesus says,

> You have heard that it was said, "*Love your neighbor* and hate your enemy." But I tell you, love your enemies and pray for those who persecute you, that you may be children of your Father in heaven (NIV, emphasis mine).

In identifying both the shalom-maker and the one who loves their enemy as God's children, Jesus creates a direct parallel. He reveals to us that while shalom-making means repairing the tears, cracks, and breaks in our society, it also means repairing those that exist in our relationships. For Jesus, shalom-making is both loving your neighbor and living with a loving disposition toward your enemy. It involves the hard work of confronting oppressive systems of injustice *and* lovingly confronting those who sinned against you. It's not neglecting the needs of the poor and abandoning your desire for revenge. It's extending mercy to those who have been wronged and to those who have wronged you by forgiving and creating space for the possibility of reconciliation. God's children do both.

Now, in all honesty, Christ's invitation to live as a shalom-maker in the world for the flourishing of my destitute neighbor is more compelling than the invitation to extend undeserved love to those who have wronged or harmed me. I'd rather be a hero than love a villain. But it makes sense that Jesus creates an intersection between shalom-making and loving one's enemy. Didn't God make shalom with His enemies through the person of Jesus Christ? Isn't our shalom a result of God's grand ability to love those who made themselves His enemies? Isn't our salvation and its resulting shalom predicated on His capacity and willingness to forgive? If so, when we, like Him, love our enemies by extending forgiveness to them, we embody Christ's shalom-making character. We prove that God is indeed our Father and that we bear His compassionate and merciful strands of DNA.

Beloved, if we are to fully enjoy the commendation of being God's children, we need to fully accept Christ's invitation to live as shalom-makers in this broken world with fallen people. We must allow the beauty of the gospel to develop within us the ability to love our enemies. We must allow the forgiveness we've received to cultivate within us the capacity to forgive. This is why Jesus, on the heels of His command to love our enemies, immediately points to the character of

God. He draws our attention away from our enemy and to the One who graciously causes the sun to shine on the righteous and unrighteous. He invites us to draw the inspiration and strength we need to be shalom-makers from the Master Shalom-Maker, who is "kind to the ungrateful and the evil" and forgives offenders (Luke 6:35).

If we are going to do the work of forgiveness, we need to be ever cognizant of the radical grace and forgiveness we've received. We need to remember the "merciful and gracious, slow to anger and abounding in steadfast love" character of God if we are to embody this character in our relationships with others (Psalm 103:8). When our flesh wants to be petty and seek revenge, we need to remember that God has not dealt with us as our sins deserve or repaid us according to our iniquities. Only the gospel will help us move in a shalom-making direction. If we do not cling to it, we will likely reject Christ's invitation to be shalom-makers and become shalom-avoidant or shalom-demanding instead.

THE DARK SIDE OF OUR
LONGING FOR SHALOM

Living as a shalom-maker in a broken world with fallen people is downright hard. You are contending not only with the self-conscious, self-centered self-preservation of others, but also with that of your own. When someone offends us, we can cover ourselves with fig leaves to cope with the pain, protect ourselves, and regain our sense of shalom. These responses are natural and are clinically referred to as defense mechanisms. They are also often warranted and worth following. In their book *The Cry of the Soul: How Our Emotions Reveal Our Deepest Questions About God*, Drs. Dan Allender and Tremper Longman further explain the value of this phenomenon that occurs within us when our shalom is fractured. Speaking specifically about fear, they write:

Fear cringes before something or someone who might hurt us physically or psychologically. We respond in flight when we view the danger as being greater than our resources and determine that self-preservation is a higher good than engagement with the danger. Fear serves a beneficial function in a fallen world. It warns us to take precautions, to hold back from certain people and situations. In this sense, fear operates analogously to pain. Pain warns us that something threatens damage to the body, and we recoil from it.

However, they quickly add that there is a "dark side" to this kind of response, saying,

Although withdrawal is frequently an appropriate response in a fallen world, fear can turn obsessive—clutching our hearts, inhibiting our activity and our enjoyment of God and His world. Instead of helping us, this kind of fear can cripple us.[1]

When someone lies, cheats, steals, betrays, or intentionally or unintentionally hurts or harms us, our natural response to recoil from the pain of offense can impair us more than help us. Our longing for shalom can become so obsessive that, instead of being shalom-makers, we become either *shalom-avoidant* or *shalom-demanding*.

Shalom-Avoidant

Those who are shalom-avoidant value cultural peace over biblical peace. Though they want their relationships to be marked by shalom, the moment their feelings of calm and tranquility start to fade, they run. For some, this running looks like sprinting away from hard conversations to "keep the peace." They think they are making shalom, but they are only stuffing and hiding. They sew fig leaves over their hurt feelings in fear that if they express them, they will be judged, rejected, or maybe further harmed. They even convince themselves that keeping their grievance and anger hidden is what Jesus meant when He called His disciples to turn the other cheek. In their biblical interpretation, keeping quiet is what it means to make shalom. But to borrow words from Dr. Tim Mackie of BibleProject: "Biblical shalom isn't the absence of conflict. It's the presence of harmony."[2]

On the other end of the shalom-avoidant spectrum are those who sprint away from relationships to "protect their peace." As soon as the relationship gets uncomfortable or requires them to do more work than they signed up for, they cancel, ghost, or find creative ways to avoid those who offend. While there can be an appropriate time to end a relationship, the shalom-avoidant defaults to quietly ghosting or harshly severing relationships when they get hard. To be fair, those who are shalom-avoidant likely have a low tolerance for emotional or relational discomfort due to past trauma or other challenging life circumstances. And sometimes, even if it might cost them a relationship, they're willing to incur the loss to preserve their peace.

Shalom-Demanding

The shalom-demanding person values retributive justice over restorative justice. Retributive justice is primarily concerned with settling debts and holding offenders accountable for their actions by prescribing a punishment that fits the crime. Its values are centered on fairness and consequences. Restorative justice is primarily concerned with repairing burned relational bridges and rehabilitating offenders. Its values are centered on mercy, second chances, and offenders taking responsibility for their actions. Both frameworks for justice are biblical, but both can be misused. In their misuse, restorative justice can give way to enabling, and retributive justice can create an opportunity for a person to become shalom-demanding. When someone wrongs them and disrupts their sense of shalom, they demand their offender restore every tear, crack, and break their sinful actions have caused. Their primary concern isn't the relationship or the rehabilitation of their offender. Their primary concern is for the person to pay them back and restore the sense of safety, security, and shalom they have lost. Their personal ethic can be summed up as an extreme version of the mantra: "No justice, no peace." Without receiving payment from their offender in the form of apologies, groveling, or retribution, forgiveness is a non-option.

The trouble with the shalom-demanding route is that it's deceptive. While you may believe and feel that you have the upper hand by making yourself the judge of your offender, you have imprisoned yourself. In demanding your offender pay up with an apology or penance, you have robbed yourself of any other pathway for living beyond their offense. If they don't say sorry and say it with the exact words or level of remorse that you long for, you refuse to be satisfied and thereby chain yourself to your unresolved anger. You think you're in control by withholding forgiveness, but you are ultimately controlled by whatever your offender does next. Now, only the offender can release you from your agony, frustration, and pain. Only their confession and repentance can restore your shalom. But if they don't confess or repent, you're left standing at a dead end, screaming out your demands with no audience. There has to be another way.

SHALOM-MAKERS IN A BROKEN
WORLD WITH FALLEN PEOPLE

In that room filled with people I admired and loved, I argued with God about what route I would take. Part of me wanted to be shalom-avoidant, pack up my dream of being a part of a multiethnic church, and leave. Another part of me wanted to be shalom-demanding, putting my "Holy Ghost filter" to the side and saying everything I had been holding in for the past few months. I was tired of being thoughtful; weary of being "eager to maintain the unity of Spirit in the bond of peace" (Ephesians 4:3). The Spirit offered me a third option, saying, "Blessed are the peacemakers, for they shall be called children of God." With His help, I lifted my eyes to meet the tearful eyes of my blood-bought sibling and entered their pain. I affirmed their experience where I could and offered an apology for where I was wrong. It was not easy. I felt like losing and dying to myself. But the Spirit quickly reminded me, "Yana, you lose nothing when you are like Jesus."

Thankfully, in this scenario, I immediately experienced the benefit of choosing the road of shalom-making. For the first time in the meeting, forward progress was made, creating space for me and others to share hard truths and be heard. As I left the meeting and debriefed with others in the parking lot, varying opinions were shared about my response. Some applauded me for extending grace. Others, with their silence, revealed their disapproval. For the next few days, I questioned my response as well. But every time I got close to wishing I had chosen another path, I was comforted once again by Jesus's words: "Blessed are the peacemakers, for they will be called children of God" (Matthew 5:9 NIV).

Beloved, if you are a follower of Jesus Christ, you are called to live as a shalom-maker in His world. This is the role you've been cast to play in God's unfolding story as you wait for Christ's return. As citizens of His Kingdom and children adopted into His family, you and I are invited to leave behind our shalom-avoidant and shalom-demanding ways and to put on the shalom-making ways of God. But this choice will be hard, often requiring you to die to comfort, preferences, and obsessive longing for shalom. As citizens of God's Kingdom who are simultaneously exiles in a broken world with fallen people, the lifestyle of a shalom-maker comes with a cost. However, living as a shalom-maker is both possible and worth it. It's possible because Jesus gives us the power and wisdom to do it. And it's worth it because every time we put aside our shalom-avoidant and shalom-demanding defense mechanisms and choose the path of shalom-making, we testify to the truth that we are God's children and receive Christ's blessed commendation: *Blessed are the shalom-makers, for they shall be called the children of God.*

SELAH: For this selah, we will meditate on the eight groups of people Jesus counts as blessed in His Sermon on the Mount in Matthew 5:3-10:

> [3] Blessed are the poor in spirit,
> for theirs is the kingdom of heaven.
> [4] Blessed are those who mourn,
> for they will be comforted.
> [5] Blessed are the meek,
> for they will inherit the earth.
> [6] Blessed are those who hunger and thirst for righteousness,
> for they will be filled.
> [7] Blessed are the merciful,
> for they will be shown mercy.
> [8] Blessed are the pure in heart,
> for they will see God.
> [9] Blessed are the peacemakers,
> for they will be called children of God.
> [10] Blessed are those who are persecuted because of righteousness,
> for theirs is the kingdom of heaven (NIV).

READ: Read Matthew 5:3-10 slowly and pause over any words or phrases that stand out to you.

REFLECT: Read Matthew 5:3-10 slowly and pause over verse 9. Consider Christ's call to be a shalom-maker. Acknowledge before Him any ways your heart may be resistant.

RESPOND: Take a moment to consider how you might need to change to live as a shalom-maker in your relationships moving forward.

- In what relationships or circumstances do you tend to be shalom-avoidant?

- In what relationships or circumstances do you tend to be shalom-demanding?

- Where do you need to heal to take up Christ's call to be a shalom-maker?

REST: Read Matthew 5:3-10 slowly again and rest in the truth that though you fall short of embodying one or more of these blessed heart postures, Christ has fulfilled them all on your behalf. Rejoice in your Savior who was poor in spirit, meek, merciful, and peace-making for your salvation.

PART 2

WHAT IS FORGIVENESS ANYWAY?

One by one they stepped to the podium and shocked the world. After two sleepless nights of tearful grieving, they extended forgiveness to a person whose hatred had altered their lives forever. Nadine Collier was the first among the family members of the Emanuel Nine to forgive Dylann Roof. Feeling ushered along by her mother's faith and love, Nadine said this, and only this, to the man who killed her mom:

> I just want everybody to know, to you, I forgive you! You took something very precious away from me. I will never be able to hold her again. But I forgive you! And have mercy on your soul. You. Hurt. Me! You hurt a lot of people. But God forgive you. And I forgive you.[1]

Next was Reverend Anthony Thompson. His wife, Myra Thompson, was leading Bible study the night Dylann Roof entered Emanuel African Methodist Episcopal Church's doors with a .45-caliber handgun and 77 bullets.[2] After forgiving Roof, Reverend Thompson offered him Christ, saying, "[My family] would like you to take this opportunity to repent. Repent. Confess. Give your life to the one who matters the most—Christ—so that he can change it, can change your ways no matter what happens to you."[3]

Watching this shocking scene play out on the news, I was utterly confused. How could they just forgive him? It hadn't even been 48 hours! Arrangements for their loved ones hadn't even been made! This man went into a church—a sacred and holy space—and coldly killed nine people during a moment of prayer. How could this be forgiven so quickly? I wanted someone to run to the microphone and yell at him. But no one did. Not even Felicia Sanders, who was in the room when it happened. Even after watching Roof bring the lives of her 26-year-old son, Tywanza Sanders, and her 87-year-old aunt, Susan Jackson, to untimely ends, she pleaded for God to have mercy on his soul.

For days, I wrestled with these quick offers of forgiveness. Were they in shock? Were they just saying what they thought God and others wanted to hear? Did they really mean it, and if so, what did it *mean* for them to forgive? Roof was in jail. They didn't have the judicial power to exonerate him of all charges. He would still undergo a trial and be held accountable for his actions. Didn't they want that? And did Reverend Anthony really want to see Dylann Roof in heaven around the throne, worshipping alongside the nations, tribes, and tongues he hated on earth? Ah, it's a beautiful sentiment and picture of the gospel, but how could they so readily forgive him? What were Sister Nadine, Revered Thompson, and Ms. Felicia actually doing when they uttered: "I forgive you"?

In this section, we are going to answer the question: What is forgiveness? Is it the work of forgetting, ignoring, and trying to change my feelings, or is it something else? I believe Jesus wants you and me to have clear answers to these questions. In the pages of Scripture, He leaves us not only *compelling whys* for forgiving others, but also *practical hows*. We will explore both, using the parable of the unforgiving servant as our guide. Since we will spend a considerable amount of time in this parable, let's take a moment to read it.

> Therefore the kingdom of heaven may be compared to a king who wished to settle accounts with his servants. When he began to settle, one was brought to him who owed him ten thousand talents. And since he could not pay, his master ordered him to be sold, with his wife and children and all that he had, and payment to be made. So the servant fell on his knees, imploring him, "Have patience with me, and I will pay you everything." And out of pity for him, the master of that servant released him and forgave him the debt. But when that same servant went out, he found one of his fellow servants who owed him a hundred denarii, and seizing him, he began to choke him, saying, "Pay what you owe." So his fellow servant fell down and pleaded with him, "Have patience with me, and I will pay you." He refused and went and put him in prison until he should pay the debt. When his fellow servants saw what had taken place, they were greatly distressed, and they went and reported to their master all that had taken place. Then his master summoned him and said to him, "You wicked servant! I forgave you all that debt because you pleaded with me. And should not you have had mercy on your fellow servant, as I had mercy on you?" And in anger his master delivered him to the jailers, until he should pay all his debt. So also my

heavenly Father will do to every one of you, if you do not forgive your brother from your heart (Matthew 18:23-35).

CHAPTER 3

FORGIVENESS IS A MERCIFUL DECISION

*Lord, how many times must I forgive my
brother or sister who sins against me?*

PETER, MATTHEW 18:21 csb

Forgiveness is referenced more than 100 times in our Bibles. After a survey of each occurrence, I have found that the Bible primarily speaks of forgiveness and its work in these three ways:

- Forgiveness is a merciful decision.

- Forgiveness is the merciful decision to release your offender of a debt.

- Forgiveness is the merciful decision to not retaliate against your offender in anger.

Together, these three biblical aspects of forgiveness can be summarized into this definition: *Forgiveness is the merciful decision to release an offender of a debt and to not retaliate against them in anger.*

In this chapter, we'll explore how mercy is at the center of the biblical definition for forgiveness. Then in the next, we'll discuss how forgiveness is the work of releasing an offender of a debt and not retaliating against them.

FORGIVENESS IS A MERCIFUL DECISION

Prior to Jesus's parable on the unforgiving servant, we find one of the most honest questions ever posed to Jesus. Peter, after hearing Jesus's teaching on how to respond to someone who has sinned against you, asks, "Lord, how many times must I forgive my brother or sister who sins against me? As many as seven times?" (Matthew 18:21 csb). Every time I read Peter's question, I'm fondly reminded of my grandmother. Ruth L. Richmond had a strict three-strikes-and-you're-out approach to forgiveness. Sis hung tough with the "fool me once" proverb. Eavesdropping on grown folks' business, I would often hear her rehearse, "Fool me once, shame on you. Fool me twice, shame on me. Fool me three times, and..." Now, it wouldn't really be appropriate for me to finish my granny's rendition of this proverb, but let's just say you didn't want to fool my granny three times. Though she was and still is the most loving and generous God-fearing person I've ever known, her patience tapped out after three rounds. Turns out, in Jesus's day, there were others who shared my grandmother's sentiments. Some rabbis even taught that God only forgives a person three times for the same sin.[1] If that's God's standard, how or even why would a human forgive more?

Peter, understanding that Jesus has come to bring about a new Kingdom, goes above the cultural norm and suggests a generous seven times. He's heard Jesus's call to love his enemies, and he's learned to pray to forgive others as he's been forgiven (Matthew 5:43-48; 6:12-15)—so he feels going seven rounds before throwing in the towel should meet Christ's standards. It's the number of completion. Seems fair. However, his suggestion doesn't even come close to the figure Jesus has in mind. Jesus responds, "I tell you, not as many as seven... but seventy times seven" (Matthew 18:22 csb). That's the standard. To help Peter understand why what appears as an inordinate suggestion is a reasonable command, Jesus shares the parable of the unforgiving servant who failed to give others the mercy he received.

What Is Mercy?

Growing up in Christendom, I often heard it said, "If grace is receiving a gift you don't deserve, mercy is not receiving the just penalty you *do* deserve." What an accessible and helpful way of describing how in Christ we receive the undeserving gift of salvation *and* escape the just penalty of death we rightly deserve. In the parable of the unforgiving servant, the first servant rightly deserves to be sold into slavery, but he receives mercy (Matthew 18:27). Instead of selling all the first servant's possessions to get at least a little bit of his money back, the master has mercy on him and forgives him of his entire ten thousand talent debt. If you're wondering how much money that is, it's about four thousand lifetimes' worth of wages![2] There is no way the servant could bring his master's account back into the black. His appeal for more time to pay off his debt is not only comical but also dishonest.

However, the master looks beyond his servant's deceptive offer, sees his desperate need, and offers mercy. At this point in Jesus's parable, I'm sure Peter, along with everyone else listening, is stunned. Who could afford to release someone of such an astronomical debt? And even if they could, who would? Doesn't the servant need to learn his lesson? And wouldn't making an example of him compel the other debtors to pay off their debts and put them on notice to not cross the master? Thankfully, the master is not a loan shark. Instead, like Jesus, he is a merciful master who forgives his offenders of a debt they could never repay. But why does he do this?

Matthew 18:27 tells us the master does this "out of pity." However, as New Testament scholar R.T. France explains, what's been translated as "out of pity" should be read as the master's "heart [going] out."[3] Where pity can carry with it the negative undertones of shame and judgment, his "heart [going] out" does not; the phrase gets us closer to understanding why the master extended such extravagant mercy and grace. This word *pity* is also often translated as "compassion" in other places throughout the New Testament.[4] In Matthew 9:36, the same word is used to describe Jesus's concern for those who were like sheep without a shepherd. In Luke 7:11-14, it is used to describe what happens inside Jesus's heart when He hears the cries of a widow walking in a funeral procession on the way to bury her son. Understanding that the life of a sonless widow living in a patriarchal society is likely to be filled with the hardship of poverty and social marginalization, Jesus is moved with compassionate concern for her future and then raises her son from the dead. This same compassionate concern fills the master's heart and compels him to forgive. It is not the kind of pity that says, "Fool me twice, shame on you." This kind of pity, birthed out of genuine concern, says, "You need help, and apart from it, you will drown—drown in your suffering, drown in your sorrow, drown in the penalty of your sin."

Later in the parable, Jesus explicitly describes the master's forgiveness of his servant's debt as an act of mercy. The Greek word here for mercy is *eleeō*, which means to help or support someone distressed and in need.[5] This definition of mercy reminds me of a hymn I often heard the seasoned saints of my childhood church singing on bended knee at Tuesday night prayer. With an intensity I'm lost for words to describe, they would sing of a God who "looked beyond all my faults and saw my need." However, what I didn't understand then that I understand now is that when the hymnist says God looks beyond our sin, it doesn't mean He ignores it. Instead, God sees my sin ever so clearly that it reveals my desperate need for help.

Beloved, God sees your sin and your need for help. With both in view, His heart goes out to you. He sees your sinful faults and knows your fallen need, and His response to both is mercy. Instead of rightfully regarding you as His enemy, He mercifully treats you as a helpless sheep in need of a Shepherd. The same is true of the merciful master who represents our merciful God in this parable. The master does not give the servant his deserved punishment. In the master's eyes, the servant is more than someone who recklessly racked up four thousand lifetimes' worth of debt. The servant is also a broken and fallen human being, who apart from the intervention of mercy and grace, will spend a lifetime (*and an eternity*) suffering under the weight of his offense. He sees his servant's debts, knows his servant's need, and meets them both with mercy.

Mercy Begets Mercy

Though not stated by the master in the story, he anticipates that his forgiven servant will be forgiving. The unspoken expectation is that his servant will joyfully extend to others the same mercy he has received. The hope is that he, too, will see his offender's faults, be understanding of the fallen need, and respond to both with mercy. Just like him, the fellow servants are fallen people living in a broken world. Just like him, they are incapable of getting it right and often get it wrong. They, too, must settle their accounts with the masters.

Three times Jesus uses the phrase "fellow servant" to describe the relationship between the first and the second servant. In doing this, Jesus is pointing out that these two men are the same. They are cut from the same self-conscious, self-centered, self-preserving cloth. They are both contending with the reality of living in a broken world with fallen people. They both need God's mercy for the forgiveness of their sin.

However, the first servant fails to remember his shared predicament with his fellow servant and treats him as an inferior. He props himself up over his fellow servant as a righteous judge demanding payment. He somehow forgets that just moments before, he was in the same humble position before his master, making the same desperate, almost word-for-word, plea. However, his fellow servant's debt was categorically different from his. Where his fellow servant owed him denarii, he owed his master talents. Where his fellow servant owed him around 6,000 dollars, he owed his master seven billion.

While his debt would take four hundred lifetimes to pay off, his fellow servant's debt would take less than four months. It was pennies in comparison to what he owed. Extending mercy to his fellow servant should have been natural and almost innate given the mercy he'd received. But blinded by his anger, he forgets the mercy he has received. He hems his brother up in a corner, cuts off the man's air supply like a loan shark, and throws him into prison.

Every time you and I choose not to do the hard work of forgiving, we are doing the shortsighted work of forgetting. We are forgetting our initial pleas for God's forgiveness when we first believed. We are forgetting a truth we must all accept: that we live in a broken world with fallen people, and that this truth calls for mercy. We are forgetting the mercy we need and the mercy we have received.

Beloved, we don't forgive because our offenders deserve it. They don't. We forgive because when we didn't, God did. Though our sin was great, He made the merciful decision to forgive, releasing us from the debt without retaliating against us in anger. In mercy, He poured out the just punishment we deserve onto His Son and extended to us mercy. How can we not freely do this given the mercy we've received?

SELAH: For this selah, let's return to Peter's question that gave way to Jesus's teaching on forgiveness in Matthew 18:21-22:

> [21] Then Peter came up and said to him, "Lord, how often will my brother sin against me, and I forgive him? As many as seven times?" [22] Jesus said to him, "I do not say to you seven times, but seventy-seven times."

READ: Read Matthew 18:21-22 slowly and pause over any words or phrases that stand out to you.

REFLECT: Read Matthew 18:21-22 again. Consider how often you have sinned against God and been met with His mercy and forgiveness. If you believe you are indeed forgiven, please pause to read and pray through 1 John 1:9, which says: "If we confess our sins, he is faithful and just to forgive us our sins and to cleanse us from all unrighteousness."

RESPOND: Read Matthew 18:21-22 slowly and pause over verse 22.

- Who do you need to forgive? If it's more than one person, list out their names.

- What do you need to forgive them of? List out their offenses against you under their names.

REST: Give thanks to God for the forgiveness you've received. Let His mercy and grace flood your heart. Only in remembering the mercy you've received can you find the will to give it. Mercy begets mercy.

CHAPTER 4

THE HARD WORK OF FORGIVENESS

Should not you have had mercy on your
fellow servant, as I had mercy on you?

JESUS, MATTHEW 18:33

The first time I read Jesus's parable of the unforgiving servant, I felt instantly convicted. The two of us had so much in common. Like him, I shortsightedly forgot the mercy I'd received. Like him, I failed to see my offender—my dad—as a fellow servant also in need of God's mercy and grace. In refusing to forgive, I had also "seized" my father by the throat, demanding he pay me back for all the pain he caused. But after reading Jesus's question at the end of the parable, I desperately wanted to release my grip and forgive. How could I withhold mercy from my dad when God had so lavishly bestowed mercy on me? My heart was ready. But I didn't know how to let go. What did it *mean* to forgive? What did it *look* and *feel* like? What was the inherent work of forgiveness?

In the last chapter, we learned from Jesus's parable that mercy is the posture we need to adopt to ready our hearts for engaging in the work of forgiveness. In this chapter, we will look at how forgiveness is addressed in other places of the Bible to better understand its twofold work—releasing an offender of a debt and not retaliating against them in anger.

FORGIVENESS IS THE MERCIFUL DECISION TO RELEASE AN OFFENDER OF A DEBT

Debt is the only analogy Jesus uses to help us discern the work of forgiveness. We find it here in Jesus's parable of the unforgiving servant and in Matthew 6:12, when He teaches His disciples to pray: "Forgive us our debts, as we also have forgiven our debtors." In Luke 7:36-50, Jesus uses His debt analogy again to confront Simon the Pharisee at a dinner party.

During the gathering, an uninvited woman with an unsavory reputation interrupts dinner and makes a scene. With an alabaster box in hand, she hurries to Jesus's feet and washes them with her tears and strands of hair. Then she anoints His feet with perfume. Simon immediately takes issue with Jesus allowing this socially unclean woman to clean His feet. Simon says to himself: "This man, if he were a prophet, would know who and what kind of woman this is who is touching him—she's a sinner!" (verse 39 CSB). Jesus, proving He is indeed a prophet, interrupts Simon's internal dialogue. Turning Simon's private conversation into a public one, Jesus presents to him this parable:

> A creditor had two debtors. One owed five hundred denarii, and the other fifty. Since they could not pay it back, he graciously forgave them both. So, which of them will love him more? (verses 41-42 CSB).

I find it profoundly interesting that financial debt is Jesus's preferred way of talking about forgiveness. *How does Jesus's debt analogy help us to better understand the work of forgiveness?* Here's my theory. When someone sins against you, they make an unauthorized withdrawal from your relational account, leaving the shared account in the red. Their offenses can also be so impactful that your personal account, which was once filled with shalom, has now been depleted by their sin, making it difficult for you and the relationship to move forward with the same ease. With our accounts in the red, we can either ignore the debt and keep pushing forward in an impoverished relationship or refuse to move forward until they bring our accounts back into the black. Instead of making the merciful decision to forgive, you can strap a workload to their backs, refusing to loosen your choke hold until they fulfill one or more of the following requirements:

- **An Apology.** You will not forgive them unless they apologize. But even if they do, their apologetic presentation must also meet your expected word count, admission of guilt, and tone.

- **An Explanation.** You will not forgive them unless they provide a reasonable explanation for the wrong they've caused. However, for some, the explanation doesn't even have to be reasonable, just understood. You can't move forward unless they explain why.

- **Shame.** Unless they are walking around filled with shame, you will not forgive them. For you, their shameful disposition says they understand the wrong they have done. You will not forgive them without seeing sorrowful evidence that they know they were wrong.

- **Groveling.** To pay off their debt, they need to woo you. You need to see them making the extra effort. Only then will you soften up and forgive.

- **They Pay You Back.** In the cases where money and material items are involved, you will not forgive them unless they pay you back.

While this list of requirements for forgiveness may seem logical, it does not match the biblical requirements for forgiveness. As we'll see later in chapter 9, while some of these are biblical requirements necessary for reconciliation, none of them are biblically required for forgiveness. Biblical forgiveness is free. Jesus required neither an apology nor an explanation to journey to Golgotha's hill for our salvation. Neither did the master in the parable of the unforgiving servant. He knew his servant's shameful groveling was insincere and still made the merciful decision to release him from paying back his debt.

This list of requirements can also lead you to a painful dead end. What if your offender refuses? What if they rip up your list of requirements and walk away? Then what? Will you allow *their* unpaid debt to leave *your* personal shalom account in the red? If you do, you will inevitably tax innocent others with the responsibility of paying your offender's debt. You will also inadvertently lock yourself in a prison and leave the key in your offender's hands. Only what *they* do next can set you free. But even if your offender meets all your requirements, you will still have to make the merciful decision to release them of their debt.

Though they offered you the apology you long for, you will have to resist the temptation to bring up old stuff moving forward. Even though they gave you a reasonable explanation for what they did, you will have to choose to not use this intel to judge, manipulate, or cancel them. When their shameful disposition clears and their groveling comes to an end, you will have to be careful not to create a new list of requirements for them to fulfill because you're still hurting. They can't move on until you're ready to move on. Plus, some offenses are so egregious that nothing your offender does can restore your shalom. The debts of betrayal, infidelity, and abuse are not easily resolved. What's lost is lost, and despite their best efforts, your offender doesn't have enough in their finite account to pay you back. The relationship only has a fighting chance at being restored if you choose to forgive, releasing them from their debt and freeing them from the responsibility to bring your account back into the black. And in many ways, your personal thriving and shalom only have a fighting chance of being restored if you choose to forgive.

However, deciding to release your offender of the responsibility is painfully difficult. Because if we do, the question is this: Who will bring my account back into the black? Friend, Christ will. He has an infinite number of resources at His disposal to heal every wound and bring your personal shalom account back into the black. His promise to all who suffer in this broken world is to, by His own hand, "restore, establish, strengthen, and support" them (1 Peter 5:10 csb). The One who calls you to make the merciful decision to release your offender of their debt will be faithful to heal you. And when you know this to be true, it makes it easier not only to mercifully release your offender of their debt, but also not retaliate against them in anger.

FORGIVENESS IS THE MERCIFUL DECISION TO NOT RETALIATE AGAINST THEM IN ANGER

In the book of Leviticus, every reference of forgiveness is mentioned alongside the sacrificial system of atonement (Leviticus 4:26; 4:31; 4:35; 5:10; 5:13; 5:16; 5:18; 6:7; 19:22). Knowing that Israel was dust and accepting the truth that they would inevitably sin against Him, God provided a way for them to maintain shalom in their relationship with Him when they messed up. He gave them the sacrificial system to atone for any intentional and unintentional sins committed against Him. For example, when a leader sinned, "doing unintentionally any one of all the things that by the commandments of the Lord his God ought not to be done," they were instructed to have a priest sacrifice the blood of a male goat on his behalf (Leviticus 4:22-26). The blood of the spotless goat atoned for the failed leader's sin, turning God's wrath away from them. After the atonement was made, the leader could be assured they were forgiven (verse 26).

Though God had established a way for Israel to maintain a right relationship with Him, Israel strayed from it. They did away with the law and the sacrificial system God had put in place for them to find their way back to Him when they messed up (2 Chronicles 35:18). As a natural consequence, God's anger burned against them. But God, being rich in mercy, offered an atoning sacrifice of His own—Jesus Christ, the righteous One (Ephesians 2:4; 1 John 2:1): "He himself [became] the atoning sacrifice for our sins, and not only for ours, but also for those of the whole world" (1 John 2:2 csb). In Christ, God extinguished His wrath toward sinners, forgiving them of their sins and providing a way for shalom to be restored in their relationship.

Beloved, this is the merciful work of forgiveness. As Christ's followers, this is the work we are called to do. With the help of the Holy Spirit, we are called to mercifully turn away from our anger and resist the desire to retaliate against those who have hurt or harmed us.

However, at times, we are guilty of being like the undeserving servant. After being forgiven of a debt he could not pay, the unforgiving servant immediately leaves the presence of his merciful master and demands his fellow servant pay the debt owed to him. Though his master's heart has gone out to him with compassion, his heart goes out to his fellow servant in anger. He violently chokes the man and throws him into prison, having quickly forgotten the mercy he's just received.

Aside from being forgetful of the mercy we've received, here are a few other reasons why we choose to retaliate against an offender in anger:

1. An idolatrous need for respect.

You refuse to let someone disrespect you and get away with it, especially if others are present. To teach your offender and your onlookers that you are not someone to be trifled with, you match your offender's energy and retaliate against them. Though your desire for others to honor you as an image-bearer is good, your desire has become inordinate, causing you to sin against God and others.[1]

2. Acute or unresolved pain.

Because the pain they cause is so unbearable, it only seems fair for the offender to be in unbearable pain as well. We refuse to suffer alone, so we retaliate against our offender to ensure their shalom is as disrupted as our own.

3. A longing for justice.

You can't live beyond offense until justice is served. You will "seize" your offender and keep your hands clasped around their throat until they receive the just punishment they deserve. Mercy is not an option. You will do whatever is in your power to make sure they pay for the pain they've caused.

When we retaliate against our offenders for any of these reasons, we bring more sin, not shalom, into the world. We return our offender's act of self-conscious, self-centered self-preservation with those of our own. We self-consciously retaliate against our offender to defend our honor. We self-centeredly allow our pain and anger to be our guide with no regard for how our actions will impact not only our offender, but also those connected to you both. Out of self-preservation, we attempt to protect our sense of shalom by seeking ultimate payment for the injustice done. But retaliation is not the way Jesus has called you and me to live beyond offense. Mercy is.

FORGIVENESS RESOLUTIONS

Nadine Collier, Reverend Anthony Thompson, and Felicia Sanders chose mercy. As an act of obedience to Christ, instead of retaliating in anger and seeking the death penalty, they objected against it. Though this was their collective work of forgiveness, to forgive Dylann Roof also meant something different for each of them.

For Nadine it meant praying for God to have mercy on Dylann's soul. For Reverend Anthony Thompson it was releasing Dylann for the insurmountable debt he owed him in the killing of his wife and offering him Jesus, the greatest treasure he had ever found. For Felicia Sanders it was treating Dylann Roof as a fellow servant. Even though she had lost so much—her son, Tywanza, and the matriarch of her family, Aunt Susie—she was committed to treating Dylann Roof as a human being created in God's image. At his penalty hearing, these were the last words she said to him: "I call you Dylann Roof," she began, "because you deserve respect—the respect you did not give Miss Susie, Reverend Clementa. You did not give respect to Sharonda Singleton...[or] Tywanza Sanders, my baby! But I'ma give you respect."[2] These were their forgiveness resolutions. This is how they defined their merciful decision to release their offender of his debt and not retaliate against him in anger.

Later in the book, you will be invited to create forgiveness resolutions of your own. But for now, selah.

SELAH: For this selah, let's return to Jesus's question for the unforgiving servant in Matthew 18:33:

> [33]Should not you have had mercy on your fellow servant,
> as I had mercy on you?

READ: Read Matthew 18:33 slowly and pause over any words or phrases that stand out to you.

REFLECT: Read Matthew 18:33 slowly. Consider the mercy you've received from Christ and what it looks like for you to extend this kind of mercy to others.

RESPOND: Consider what your greatest barriers are to making the merciful decision to release your offender of their debt and not retaliate against them in anger.

- What's on your list of requirements they need to fulfill for you to forgive? Is it an apology, explanation, a shameful disposition, groveling, or something else?

- What do you think fuels your desire to retaliate against someone who has sinned against you? Is it your pain, a need for respect, a longing for justice, or something else?

REST: Read Matthew 18:33 slowly. Even though you may not be ready to forgive and extend to others the mercy you've received, sit with this truth. Ask God to soften your heart, making it merciful like His. Rest in His promise that if you ask anything in agreement with His will, He will hear us and do as we asked (1 John 5:14).

CHAPTER 5

FORGIVENESS IS NOT FORGETTING

You will cast all our sins into the depths of the sea.

MICAH 7:19

B esides being unable to easily resolve my anger and not knowing what forgiveness truly was, the other great barrier to forgiving my dad was failing to understand what forgiveness was *not*. Cultural mantras like "forgive and forget" had me thinking the work of forgiveness was the work of forgetting. A surface-level reading of Jesus's command to turn the other cheek and to love one's enemy led me to conclude that forgiveness was a matter of ignoring what happened and cheerfully pressing on. Jesus's requirement to forgive from the heart left me feeling defeated. What if I couldn't ever replace my feelings of anger with tranquil, loving ones? *What* was forgiveness and *how* would I do it? At this point in my life, I was a long way from understanding forgiveness is *the merciful decision to release an offender of a debt and not retaliate against them in anger.* But I was faithfully trying—trying to forget, trying to ignore, and trying to force my feelings to change. However, with each try, I found myself confronted with a dead end.

Perhaps you've also encountered one or more of these dead ends. You want to forgive but trying to forget, ignore, and change your feelings isn't working. If so, in the final chapters of this section, I want to invite you to trade the futile work of forgetting, ignoring, and trying to change your feelings for the fruitful work of *faithfully casting, humbly confronting*, and *decisively committing*. Let's start with the dead end of forgetting.

FORGIVENESS IS NOT FORGETTING

Forgive and forget was not just a mantra I picked up from the culture. It was also a creed I learned in church. Growing up Black and Christian, I had grown accustomed to the end of a sermon, regardless of its text, ascending to a victorious retelling of Jesus's blood shed at Calvary. Queuing the organist to join them, the preacher would start to whoop, singing, "Ohhhh! But when I turn my eyes to Calvary! I see a man named Jesus hanging on a tree for you and me!" People would begin to stand to their feet. To encourage more to do the same, the preacher would take it up an octave and say, "But that's not how the story ends! Three days later, He rose from the dead with all power in His nail-scarred hands!" I can hear and even feel the congregation's praise-filled response now as I think back to all those Sunday mornings and afternoons spent in church. What a gift to hear the gospel proclaimed week after week.

Every now and then, the preacher might add to their jubilant recounting of Christ's death on the cross: "God has thrown all of our sins into the sea of forgetfulness." Though I'd heard this refrain said several times by various preachers in different denominations, I had no idea where these words were in my Bible. But I was certain, given the consensus among preachers, that this was a direct quote from Scripture. And almost every time I heard it, I would mentally leave the room. Though I found the idea of God throwing my sins into the sea of forgetfulness immensely beautiful, it distracted my worship and sent my intellectual wheels turning. It drew up some questions for me:

- How can an all-knowing God forget? Sure, He can do any-thing. But isn't the essence of being all-knowing to know all things? How is this theologically possible?

- If forgetting is what it means to forgive, what happens if I can't forget? While I was completely on board with the selective amnesia plan, how does someone erase the pains of abuse, abandonment, infidelity, and betrayal from their core memory?

Why Forgetting Is a Dead End

Forgetting can be a dead end for anyone truly trying to forgive. Here are three reasons why:

1. Forgetting is not always possible.

Some memories will never fade. They are so embedded into our storyline that even when we aren't thinking about the offense or trauma we've experienced, we're still living in response to it. Even if our offender is long gone or not in close enough proximity to phys-ically or emotionally hurt us again, we can be anxious, emotionally detached, and just so dang angry all the time. While the offense is no longer front of mind, our body has stored the anniversaries of when the pain of someone else's self-centered choices entered our life and sends trigger warnings when it perceives a familiar threat. Forgetting is not always possible.

2. Forgetting the past is not always in touch with the reality of the present.

If the person who has offended you doesn't turn over a new leaf, you will struggle to forget the past. Their repeated offenses make forgiving-as-forgetting a non-option. Were you to try to forget and turn the page, you wouldn't find a new chapter. Instead, you would find the same story and sinful behaviors. Also, if we ignore the present in our attempts to forget the past, we will open ourselves up to more harm. But as we will see in the next chapter, Christ's call to forgive is not a call to open yourself up to further harm. It is a call to be in touch with reality and humbly confront it.

3. Forgetting can be shalom-avoidant.

The shalom-avoidant person stuffs, hides, and sweeps grievances under the rug in the name of peacekeeping. Because they hate conflict, they can cling to the forgive-and-forget mantra to escape having a hard yet necessary conversation. They would prefer to keep the peace than to speak up. But, as we saw in chapter 2, biblical peace—shalom—is not the absence of conflict. It's the presence of harmony. Those who choose forgetting as their path to forgiveness will only gain a faux sense of harmony and will have to keep stuffing, hiding, and sweeping to maintain it. This is even true when your offender is long gone or far away. If you concentrate all your effort on suppressing your feelings and forgetting your trauma, you will reach a dead end and not be able to restore shalom within yourself. The road to shalom and forgiveness starts with honestly acknowledging your offender's sin and the pain it caused—not forgetting it.

TRADE FORGETTING
FOR FAITHFULLY CASTING

If forgiving doesn't mean forgetting, then what do we do with the preacher's words: "God has thrown all of our sins into the sea of forgetfulness." As followers of Jesus Christ, aren't we expected to follow His model for forgiveness? Well, yes, but the preacher's words are a misquote. Micah 7:19 reads, "[God] will cast all our sins into the depths of the sea," not "God will cast all our sins into the sea *of forgetfulness.*" No translation is written this way. However, I do understand how the preachers in my home church reached this interpretation. In Jeremiah

31:34, God tells Israel that despite their egregious record of abominations against Him, He will "forgive their iniquity" and "remember their sin no more." But, once again, *how can an all-knowing God forget?* I love the sentiment, but I'm not sure a forgetful God is what we want. What else is He bound to forget? My prayer requests? His promises? The offenses that were committed against me? No, thank you. I want and need a God whose memory is fully intact.

Thankfully, this is the God we have. When the Bible speaks of God forgetting or remembering, it doesn't imply there is ever a time when His knowing has fallen short of all-knowing. Instead, the Bible is using anthropomorphic language, ascribing finite human characteristics to an infinite God, to help us get a sense of what God and His activity in the world are like. In the same way a school teacher uses age-appropriate analogies and language to help a child's developing brain grasp an idea that's a wee bit beyond their reach, God uses human language and experiences to help us understand infinite truths about Him. When God says He will forget, He is assuring us His forgiveness of sin will hold. Though He cannot forget, He will *relate* to us as if He did. Just as you can trust a forgetful person to not recall the details of the past, you can trust God to not bring up old stuff. He will not dangle offenses over your head or throw the past in your face. "As far as the east is from the west," so far will He "remove our transgressions from us" (Psalm 103:12). He *faithfully casts* your offenses along with His wrath into the depths of the sea. *He doesn't forget; He casts.*

As believers, this is the model of forgiveness we are called to follow. We need to trade forgetting for the work of faithfully casting. And it will be work. However, for our most intimate relationships to survive offense, we must do this work. Like God, we will need to cast our offender's sin against us into the depths of the sea and relate to them as if we have no memory of the wrong they have done. Every time their offense creeps back into the memories of our bodies and minds, we will need to resist the urge to throw our fishing rod back into the depths of the sea to draw them back up. Instead, with each recurring reminder of their offense, we will, with God's help, live out our committed decision to forgive and faithfully recast their *forgiven sin* into the depths of the sea. Emphasis on *forgiven sin*.

If someone commits a new offense of a similar kind or continues to behave in a manner that deems them emotionally and physically unsafe, confronting them about their sin isn't bringing up old stuff. It's addressing a pattern. Though you are still called to do the work of forgiveness for their new offense or offenses (that 77 times is real!), you do have the freedom to confront them about their sin, hold them accountable to change, and restructure the relationship if they don't. But if the person has demonstrated remorse and repented of their past offenses, when they inevitably commit a new one because they are human, we relate to them concerning this new offense as if we have no memory of the old. We are careful to not bring past forgiven sin into the present. We make the merciful and committed decision to not bring up old stuff.

This work of faithfully casting reminds me a lot of our committed decision to follow Jesus. In Luke 9:23, Jesus says to all who wish to follow Him, "If anyone would come after me, let him deny himself and take up his cross daily and follow me." Jesus's use of the word *daily* implies that though every disciple will make the onetime life-altering decision to deny themselves and take up their cross to follow Him, they will have to recommit to that decision daily. Every morning and in every moment of adversity, they will have to decide whether they will continue to carry their cross or set it aside. The same is true with forgiveness. When we forgive, we make the one-time merciful decision to release our offender of their debt and not retaliate against them. However, when we wake in the morning and our minds or bodies are flooded once again with the memories of the pain caused, we faithfully cast our urge to seek retribution or retaliation back into the depths of the sea and recommit to our decision to forgive. With God's help, we daily pick up our cross and follow Jesus down the road of forgiveness.

SELAH: For this selah, let's sit with Micah 7:18-19:

> [18] Who is a God like you, pardoning iniquity
> and passing over transgression
> for the remnant of his inheritance?
> He does not retain his anger forever,
> because he delights in steadfast love.
>
> [19] He will again have compassion on us;
> he will tread our iniquities underfoot.
> You will cast all our sins
> into the depths of the sea.

READ: Read Micah 7:18-19 slowly and pause over any words or phrases that stand out to you.

REFLECT: Read Micah 7:18-19 slowly. Consider how God has pardoned your iniquity and lavished His compassion on you.

RESPOND: Consider how you need to trade forgetting for faithfully casting.

- Are you trying to forget any sins committed against you?
- Are there any forgiven sins that you draw up often? If so,

with whom and under what circumstances do you tend to draw them up?

- What does it practically look like for you to faithfully cast the sin committed against you into the depths of the sea?

———————————

REST: The work of faithfully casting is difficult, especially when your wounds are fresh and the person who offended you lives in your home or is part of your weekly rhythm. You will need God's help. Rest now in the truth that you have 24-hour access to God through prayer. If you're a believer, His Spirit lives within you. If at any point you need His help to faithfully cast your offender's forgiven sin back into the sea, He is there.

CHAPTER 6

FORGIVENESS IS NOT IGNORING

If anyone slaps you on the right cheek,
turn to him the other also.

JESUS, MATTHEW 5:39

In 2020, Nigerian-American hip-hop artist Tobe Nwigwe unapolo-getically said out loud what many people throughout history have quietly said to themselves upon hearing Jesus's instruction to turn the other cheek (Matthew 5:38-39). In the wake of the deaths of Breonna Taylor, Elijah McClain, and George Floyd and what felt like calls for Christians to ignore injustice for the sake of unity, Nwigwe sent out this public service announcement: "Try Jesus, not me." As a Chris-tian, Nwigwe sought to be a peaceful man, but if someone harmed him or his family, he wouldn't be turning the other cheek like Jesus commanded. Things were bound to get physical.

Since I'm not a skilled fighter and throwing hands would likely result in me hitting myself, it would be unwise for me to put out this kind of PSA. However, like Nwigwe, I struggle with Jesus's turn-the-other-cheek theology. When I get to this part of Jesus's inaugural ser-mon, my amens also begin to fade. *Jesus, do You really want me to get slapped again?* Why does Jesus's command read "If someone slaps you, turn the other cheek" and not "If someone slaps you, walk away"? I can get down with walking away. I can accept and apply that, but why stay?

Though much of the Bible can be readily understood, some passages require a kind of archaeological dig. Jesus's teaching on cheek-turning is one of them. You've got to pull out some commentaries to dig up the historical, cultural, and social contexts. You've got to do some word studies to examine how our English definitions compare with those of the original Hebrew or Greek. And sometimes you've got to consider the whole counsel of Scripture and ask the question: What *couldn't* this mean?

WHAT JESUS DOESN'T MEAN

In light of His character and the whole counsel of Scripture, here's what Jesus couldn't mean when He commands us to turn the other cheek:

1. To willfully allow someone to continuously sin against you.

Remember, Jesus hates sin. Whether you are the one sinning against someone or someone is sinning against you, Jesus hates it. If someone's lying tongue betrays you or wicked heart abuses you, Jesus would not be on board with them doing further harm. He came to rid the world of sin, not to promote it. He came to establish a new Kingdom filled with shalom, not more sin. If turning the other cheek means willfully allowing someone to continuously sin against you, this creates more opportunity for sin to flourish. This is the antithesis of shalom. But Jesus and His teachings are meant to be a conduit of more shalom, not more sin—so turning the other cheek can't mean staying and letting someone continue to abuse or sin against you. It must mean something else.

2. To ignore sin.

Turning the other cheek also can't be a call to ignore sin. Nowhere in Scripture do we see God, the Father, the Son, or the Holy Spirit ignoring sin. The triune God ain't no Swiffer Sweeper. When Israel sinned against Him, God sent prophets to confront them about their sin and plead with them to turn back to Him. The Holy Spirit's chief responsibility is to "convict the world concerning sin" (John 16:8), and I can personally testify that He is very good at doing His job. And through His teaching, Jesus is faithful to do the same. Prior to His command to turn the other cheek, Jesus calls out those who have proverbially slapped their neighbors' cheeks with insults. He says to them, "You have heard that it was said to those of old, 'You shall not murder; and whoever murders will be liable to judgment.' But I say to you that everyone who is angry with his brother will be liable to judgment; whoever insults his brother will be liable to the council" (Matthew 5:21-22). Jesus doesn't overlook their sinful anger or insults; He rebukes them. *He doesn't ignore sin; He confronts it.* And, as His followers, He calls us to do the same.

TRADE IGNORING FOR
HUMBLY CONFRONTING

Cards on the table. I believe Jesus's command to turn the other cheek is not a command to ignore an offense, but to *humbly confront* it. Stay with me though. We've got a lot of ground to cover to find our way to this truth. Let's start by reading Jesus's command.

> You have heard that it was said, "An eye for an eye and a
> tooth for a tooth." But I say to you, Do not resist the one
> who is evil. But if anyone slaps you on the right cheek,
> turn to him the other also" (Matthew 5:38-39).

In these verses, Jesus is zeroing in on the Jewish law of retribution. This is the fifth of six Jewish laws Jesus reexamines. Prior to touching on the law of retaliation, Jesus addresses those pertaining to murder, adultery, divorce, and oath-taking. However, Jesus isn't reexamining the laws because something is wrong with them or because He wants to do away with them. Instead, He's calling Israel to take a closer look at these six laws because they have become lax in their interpretation of and obedience to them (Matthew 5:19-20). For them, obedience was primarily about checking boxes and staying out of trouble with God, not a way to cultivate shalom with God and neighbor. They knew the law, but they missed the heart—the intent—of it. With each reexamination of these laws, Jesus clarifies that sin isn't merely a behavior. It's also the perverse longings of the heart.

They had heard it said, "Whoever murders will be liable to judgment," but they missed the need to extinguish anger and bitterness in their hearts. They understood they shouldn't have sex with someone who wasn't their spouse, but they missed that adultery doesn't start and end with lying with someone other than your spouse. It starts with looking at someone for a little too long and allowing lust to take root in your heart. The written law allowed a man to divorce his wife if he found "some indecency in her" (Deuteronomy 24:1), but their religious leaders had stretched the meaning of indecency, saying a man could divorce his wife if he was displeased with her housekeeping, attractiveness, cooking skills, or sexual performance.

This kind of relaxed, loophole-finding interpretation of the law also found its home in Israel's laws of retribution. As a principle for how to settle civil disputes, God had these laws written in His covenant with Israel:

> Whoever takes a human life shall surely be put to death. Whoever takes an animal's life shall make it good, life for life. If anyone injures his neighbor, as he has done it shall be done to him, fracture for fracture, eye for eye, tooth for tooth; whatever injury he has given a person shall be given to him (Leviticus 24:17-20).

Though it was rare for someone to literally exchange an eye for an eye or a tooth for a tooth, the heart of the law was to restore shalom in the wake of offense. But restoration wasn't the only reason God put these laws in place.

God, in His wisdom, also put these laws in place to act as guardrails. He knows our hearts are bent toward self-conscious, self-centered self-preservation. He knows that in the wake of offense, we are liable to demand more recompense from our offenders than what is fair. He knows we will be tempted to seek not only justice but also revenge.

Likewise, Israel failed to allow the law of retribution to retrain their urge to retaliate against their offender; instead, they used the law to fuel it. They ignored God's command—"You shall not take vengeance or bear a grudge against the sons of your own people, but you shall love your neighbor as yourself: I am the Lord"—and sought as much vengeance possible (Leviticus 19:18).

Into this misuse and twisting of God's law, Jesus calls them back to the heart of it. He says, "You have heard that it was said, 'An eye for an eye and a tooth for a tooth.' *But I say to you, Do not resist the one who is evil*" (Matthew 5:38-39, emphasis mine). When we read Jesus's command "do not resist," it's easy to think Jesus is calling us to give in or surrender to the demands or abuse of an evil person—to just let it happen without protest. However, Jesus's command isn't a call to acquiesce to abuse or be a doormat for the glory of His name. Jesus's command is a call to resist your inward inclination to retaliate. In the Greek, the phrase that's been translated in our Bible as "do not resist" would've been heard as "do not be hostile toward" or "do not set oneself against" by Jesus's audience.[1] But if I may translate it for us into our modern-day vernacular, Jesus is essentially saying, "Don't square up!" "Do not resist" is not a call to match the self-conscious, self-centered, self-persevering energy of your offender. It's a call to not be shalom-demanding with hearts set on getting our offender back. It's a call to lay down our desire to avenge ourselves and entrust our offenders to the will of God. This is the ideal response of those who call Jesus "Lord" and are citizens of His Kingdom.

Jesus goes on to add, "If anyone slaps you on the right cheek, *turn to him the other also*" (Matthew 5:39, emphasis mine). A first-century Jew would have immediately associated someone being slapped on the right cheek with someone being slapped with the back of the hand. In every century, a backhanded slap is highly offensive, but in a Jewish honor and shame culture, it is one of the highest forms of humiliation. Rabbis equated this slap to spitting on a person, pulling off their clothing, or loosing a woman's hair in public.[2] It was a degrading form of abuse not only for inflicting harm but also for disrobing a person of their inherent dignity and worth. It was a shaming tactic—a demoralizing offense. In Jesus's context, this was the kind of slap a master would give a slave to remind them of their social rank. It was the master's way of putting their slave back into their place, to say with the sting of their backhand, "You ain't on my level. Never have been. Never will be." However, on other occasions, someone would use this degrading form of abuse to bully, humiliate, or assert their power over an enemy. Usually, the retribution required for this offense was a monetary fine twice that of an openhanded slap.[3] But Jesus, understanding that consequences don't always change hearts, offers a more restorative solution.

When Jesus tells His disciples to turn the other cheek, He is commanding them to humbly confront their offender by inviting them to reexamine the hierarchy they've created in their mind and to treat them as a fellow image-bearer. Dr. Tim Mackie of BibleProject explains,

> Not walking away, but standing right there, and then, just, looking in the eyes of the person that [backhand slapped you], and then offering them your other cheek isn't doing nothing. What you are requiring them to do is slap you

again. But this time with an open hand…an open palm slap is symbolic of a social equal.[4]

Turning the other cheek was meant to be a nonviolent, creative response that sent a shockwave through your offender's conscience, reminding them you are both created in the image of God. It was a way to say without words or fists, "I am on your level. Always have been. Always will be." For an enslaved person, it was their way of saying to their master, "Though we rank differently in society, we share the same rank before God. We are both image-bearers worthy of dignity, honor, and respect." While they could get slapped again, at least this time, with their right cheek protected, it would be an openhanded slap among equals. And in a shame and honor culture, this would've restored the humiliated person's dignity and removed their shame. Very rarely would a backhanded slapper RSVP to this invitation. Instead, they would perceive such a gesture as an act of defiance. *How dare you suggest we are equals? How dare you judge my actions as unjust?* They would've preferred to pay the fine and leave their enemy suffering humiliation than to slap them on the other cheek. That would've felt too much like an empowering apology because by doing so they would be admitting their actions were unjust, thereby restoring the person's dignity. And herein lies the reason why Jesus doesn't tell His disciples to walk away, but to stand ten toes down and offer them the other cheek.

Walking away would've been ignoring, and ignoring sin and wrongs committed against you doesn't lead to heart transformation. But as Jesus has already demonstrated in His teachings on anger, lust, and divorce, heart transformation is His target. His goal and the goal of His commands is to shepherd our hearts away from their perverse longings to righteous shalom-making ones. If, after being shamed, you simply walked away from your offender, they would continue to live under the presumptive lie that they are more deserving of dignity, honor, and respect than others. But by turning the other cheek, you humbly confront your offender's sin against you. You invite them to repent of their superiority complex and build a relationship with you marked by a mutual love and respect for one another.

Before we move to the next chapter, I want to address those whose offenders are long gone or not safe to contact. You may never be able to humbly confront them for the sin they caused against you, but that doesn't leave you without a pathway out of the dead end of ignoring. It may be alluring to suppress and ignore the trauma you've experienced, but if you don't honestly acknowledge it, the trauma will continue to hold you captive. I know. It isn't fair. You didn't ask for it, but the only way you can find your way out is to be honest about what happened. We will talk more about how to live beyond the offenses of abuse in part 4, but for now, let's selah.

SELAH: For this selah, let's sit with Jesus's teaching on turning the other cheek in Matthew 5:38-42:

> [38] You have heard that it was said, "An eye for an eye and a tooth for a tooth." [39] But I say to you, Do not resist the one who is evil. But if anyone slaps you on the right cheek, turn to him the other also. [40] And if anyone would sue you and take your tunic, let him have your cloak as well. [41] And if anyone forces you to go one mile, go with him two miles. [42] Give to the one who begs from you, and do not refuse the one who would borrow from you.

READ: Read Matthew 5:38-42 slowly and pause over any words or phrases that stand out to you.

REFLECT: Read Matthew 5:38-42 slowly. Consider your immediate reaction to Jesus's command to turn the other cheek and how it might be shifting as you better understand what Jesus meant.

RESPOND: Consider how to apply Jesus's teaching.

- On a scale of 1–10, how comfortable are you with confronting others? Consider what experiences, fears, or beliefs inform your comfort level.

- Is there anyone in your life you need to humbly confront and can do so safely?

- Have any sins been committed against you that you have trouble honestly acknowledging? If so, why are they hard to acknowledge?

REST: Though humbly confronting others is difficult and the outcome of doing so is always uncertain, rest in this truth: "Blessed are the [shalom-makers], for they will be called children of God" (Matthew 5:9 NIV).

CHAPTER 7

FORGIVENESS IS NOT A FEELING

Forgive your brother or sister from your heart.

JESUS, MATTHEW 18:35 NIV

As someone who registers as a high feeler on almost every personality test on the market, when I encountered Jesus's command to forgive from the heart, I felt doomed to fail. If forgiving was a matter of changing my feelings, this was bad news for me. Historically, emotions often sit on the judge's bench of my heart, setting the direction for my decision-making. Logic is hardly given an opportunity to sway my feelings toward considering more evidence. Past experiences aren't readily invited to present opposing arguments to round out my feelings. And sometimes, even the truth doesn't get an opportunity to take the stand. What I *feel* is the truth, and you would be hard-pressed to convince me otherwise.

My feelings can have this same controlling power even when they are absent. When the desire to work out is lacking, I'm less likely to put on my gym shoes and give my body what it needs. When a healthy concern about how I spend money is nonexistent, I fail to budget and "ball out" even though my income is clearly saying, "Girl, we need to stay in!" And, when my anger morphs into apathy and indifference, leaving my heart devoid of compassion, mercy, and love, I am less likely to forgive.

THE EVOLUTION OF EMOTIONS

Data shows that my emotion-based decision-making process isn't just a matter of my God-given makeup. It's also the product of my social conditioning. According to Harvard's 2014 *Annual Review of Psychology* report: "Emotions are, for better or worse, the dominant driver of most meaningful decisions in life."[1] However, this is not how it's always been, and it wasn't until the late 1990s and early 2000s that emotions played a predominant role in decision-making across Western cultures.[2] Psychologist and expert in generational differences Dr. Jean Twenge provides some context for this change. In her book *Generations: The Real Differences Between Gen Z, Millennials, Gen X, Boomers, and Silents*, she explains that prior to emotions being the dominant drivers in decision-making, the cultural values were sacrificing "for the greater good" and "rule-following."[3] However, over time the cultural value of sacrificing one's comfort, success, and preference for the greater good was traded for being one's authentic, unconstrained self. According to her research, "do your own thing" became the new driver of decision-making in the 1960s, and in the 1980s it was joined by the cultural mantra to "just be yourself."[4] Over the past decade, "do what feels good," "good vibes only," and "be the main character in your story" have joined the list of cultural mantras that have become the moral compasses and primary drivers in decision-making processes. Dr. Karl Moore, another psychologist and expert in generational differences, offers this explanation for the shift:

> [Millennials] want to be able to be themselves. They are not interested in playing "the game" their parents once did. For many Boomers, the cost of playing "the game" was too high: failed marriages, too much travel, too little work-life balance, etc.[5]

Real talk. Moore ain't lying. Millennials are not for playing "the game," saving face, or being politically correct to appease leadership structures that need to be amended. If the rule doesn't make sense, we are bound to challenge it. We pride ourselves on being a more liberated generation than our foreparents. However, as much as we may not want to be like our parents, we must acknowledge and thank them for how their other-centered rule-following created space for our out-of-the-box thinking to thrive. We must also acknowledge that though we've swung the pendulum in the opposite direction to bring more balance, we have pridefully overcorrected.

While we may not be doing things their way, our way has also led to failed marriages, too much travel, and too little work-life balance. Doing what feels right, in the spirit of keeping it 100, has led to broken relationships that could've been mended with more mercy, patience, and care. Our priority to protect one's peace has led to more travel, entertainment, and treats than reasonable to escape and replace unpleasant emotions. Our often-untamed entrepreneurialism and hustle culture has burnt us out as well, necessitating the rise of the self-care movement and the church's return to more faithfully practicing the Sabbath. Our feelings-based decision-making model has also, in my opinion, presented as our greatest barrier to obeying Jesus's command to forgive.

WHY FEELINGS CAN BE DEAD ENDS
1. Feelings can be stubborn.

Our emotions are more than sensations that radiate through our bodies. They are expressions intricately connected to our values, beliefs, and loves. Because these three are often fixed constructs of our personhood, when they are broken, rejected, or offended, we feel. For one person, this primary feeling may be anger. For another, it may be sadness, anxiety, or apathy. Depending on the degree of the offense and your attachment to your values, beliefs, and loves, these feelings won't easily budge. And if your obedience to Christ's command to forgive is predicated on your feelings, you won't budge either.

2. Feelings can be fickle.

As stubborn as feelings can be, they can also be fickle, taking you and the people in your life on an emotionally exhausting and relationally stifling roller coaster. When the endorphins are poppin' and your spirit is still reveling in Sunday's service, you are more inclined to love your neighbor, look out for the interests of others, and live peaceably with those you don't like. But when the troubles of betrayal, slander, or disappointment come into your life, obedience begins to wane. What God declares is good gets replaced with what feels good. What's God-glorifying gets traded for the path of least resistance. God's call to shalom-making loses its allure, and we become shalom-avoidant or shalom-demanding.

3. Feelings can cause us to stray from God and His ways.

A feelings-based decision-making model may yield instant gratification, but it will not yield lasting God-honoring fruit. Jesus alerts every man or woman who desires to follow Him of this reality, saying: "If anyone would come after me, let him deny himself and take up his cross and follow me" (Matthew 16:24). Sometimes our obedience to Christ will require us to work against the grain of our feelings. And we will almost always have to go against the grain of what we feel to obey Jesus's command to forgive.

Though feelings can be a dead end, they are not the enemy. Feelings are good! They are beautiful and helpful God-given gifts. In their book *Untangling Emotions*, Christian counselors J. Alasdair Groves and Winston T. Smith point out that our emotions are meant to help us *communicate* what we value, *connect* us to others, *motivate* us to action, and *turn* us toward God. They also explain that though the origin of our emotions is important, God is more concerned with "what our emotions do" and "where they lead us."[6] Does our fear for the health of a relationship lead us to humbly confront offenses or sweep them under the rug? Does our love for someone lead us to stay long enough to see if trust can be rebuilt, or does it lead us to haphazardly and prematurely end the relationship to protect ourselves from getting hurt? Is your anger a cue to turn toward God on bended knee and pour out your heart to Him, or does your anger compel you to stand up against your offender to get them back?

While our feelings can be the very thing that derails us from obeying God, they possess within them the potential to motivate us toward Him and His ways. Feelings are good. However, God will call us at times to resist what we feel for His glory and His definition of the greater good—shalom. But what I love most about Jesus is that He is always willing to go first. He is not a "do as I say, not as I do" kind of rabbi. He is a "come and follow Me" kind of rabbi.

JESUS, OUR EXAMPLE

In the Garden of Gethsemane, Jesus had some *big* feelings. He is in pain, emotionally, physically, and even spiritually. In Mark 14:33-34, Jesus is described as "greatly distressed" and "troubled." He even confesses to Peter, James, and John that His "soul is very sorrowful." Though He came into the world to die for sinners and has even prophesied of His certain death, now that His hour has come, He prays for an alternate route. In agony, with "sweat like great drops of blood falling down to the ground," He cries out: "My Father, if you are willing, remove this cup from me. Nevertheless, not my will, but yours, be done" (Luke 22:41-44).

This picture of Jesus in utter emotional, physical, and spiritual pain as He counts up the cost of humanity's forgiveness gives us more clarity on what Jesus means when He instructs His disciples to forgive from the heart (Matthew 18:35). It can't mean waiting for your feelings to blossom into a desire to obey. It can't mean feeling your way to obedience. Why? Because even though Jesus's soul is "greatly distressed" and "troubled" at the coming of His certain death, He chooses to not surrender to the will of His feelings and instead surrenders Himself to the will of God. Even though His soul was "very sorrowful," He forfeits His desire for comfort and safety and decisively commits to drinking the cup of suffering and death for your forgiveness and mine. He goes against the grain of what He feels in service of God's greater good—our salvation.

Now to be clear, Jesus doesn't resist the pull of His feelings by ignoring them. In Mark 14:34, He confesses to His disciples, "My soul is very sorrowful, even to death." And as we've already seen, He doesn't hold His feelings back or restrain His tears in any way during His time of prayer before God. He honestly acknowledges His feelings; He just doesn't obey them. He doesn't allow His feelings to sit on the judge's bench of His heart, dictating His decision-making. When the time comes for Him to stop praying for a different answer and to surrender His body to the Father's will, He gets up and says to His disciples: "See, the hour is at hand, and the Son of Man is betrayed into the hands of sinners. Rise, let us be going; see, my betrayer is at hand" (Matthew 26:45-46). He decisively commits.

TRADE FEELINGS FOR
DECISIVELY COMMITTING

When we encounter the word *heart* in the Bible, we must be careful to not read our twenty-first-century Western definition into it. While the biblical definition of heart includes feelings, its meaning encompasses so much more. The Greek word used here for *heart* is *kardia*, which also includes one's desires, intellect, and volition.[7] This heart is the place where feelings are felt, beliefs and values are formed, and commitments are made. Now, in a perfect world, all three of these would always work together in harmony, but in our broken world, this is not always the case. Many people at the start of any given year make the commitment to work out, eat clean, and drink more water. They make this commitment based on the belief that their health is important, and if they don't steward it well, it can lead to adverse consequences. They start out well. But if their feelings have faded, so does their commitment. However, their beliefs haven't changed. And the question they're faced with as they decide whether they'll get back on the wagon is: Will they obey what they feel or what they believe?

This is often the question we encounter daily in the Christian life. Will we obey our feelings, or will we obey God? It is also the question we struggle to answer when we're offended, angry, or in pain. Will you, like our Savior, decisively commit to do the hard work of forgiveness, or will you cancel them or seek revenge?

Beloved, making the merciful and committed decision to forgive those who have sinned against you is one of Jesus's hardest teachings to obey. Everything in you wants to run in the opposite direction or bulldoze headfirst into the person who hurt you. This is our natural inclination. But praise God for His Spirit that abides within, empowering us to not give in to the inclination of our flesh, and instead follow Christ's way of mercy and forgiveness even when our feelings aren't on board.

As a super-feeler with stubborn feelings toward my dad, I wasn't sure if my feelings of anger and apathy would ever turn warm and fuzzy. For the longest time, I felt an enormous amount of guilt and shame. My lack of joy and excitement at the sight of his calls caused me to question whether I had truly forgiven him. I was praying and doing my best to bite my tongue, but my anger wasn't readily going away. And if my feelings were the measure for determining if I had indeed forgiven my dad from the heart, I was failing. But, as we've

seen in this section, this is not what Jesus means when He commands His followers to forgive from the heart. Forgiveness is not a
feeling; it's a choice. It's the merciful decision to release an offender
of their debt and to not retaliate against them, even though they
don't deserve it. If you, like me, are a super-feeler, I pray this truth
gives you comfort and direction. You don't have to wait for your
feelings to catch up to follow Jesus's command to forgive. Instead,
when feelings are lacking, you can, as an exercise of your God-given
free will, *decisively commit*.

We've covered a lot of ground in this section. Here is a chart to
help summarize what the work of forgiveness is and is not.

Three Dead Ends to Forgiveness	Three Fruitful Pathways to Forgiveness
Forgiveness is forgetting.	Forgiveness is faithfully casting.
Forgiveness is ignoring.	Forgiveness is humbly confronting.
Forgiveness is a feeling.	Forgiveness is decisively committing.

SELAH: For this selah, let's sit with the last words from Jesus's parable of the unforgiving servant in Matthew 18:35 (ERV):

> 35 You must forgive your brother or sister with all your heart.

READ: Read this verse slowly and pause over any words or phrases
that stand out to you.

REFLECT: Read this verse slowly. Consider which of the dead ends
of forgetting, ignoring, and feeling you run into the most. If none of

these describes your dead ends, consider other ones you find yourself running into. Name them.

RESPOND: Slowly read this verse again. Ask God to help you honestly answer these questions.

- On a scale of 1–10—1 meaning "not at all" and 10 meaning "all the time"—how much of a role do your emotions play in your decision-making?

- What feelings do you need to bring under Jesus's command to decisively commit to forgiving those who've sinned against you? List them out.

REST: Rest and rejoice in your God who faithfully cast your sin into the depths of the sea, humbly confronted your offenses against Him by sending His Son, Jesus, into the world to die for your sins, and then decisively committed to forgiving you by sealing you with His Holy Spirit. Rest and trust that as you rejoice in this truth, God's Spirit will inspire and empower you to extend to others the mercy you've received.

PART 3

JESUS CULTURE

Worldviews matter. Everyone has one. However, many of us live unaware of who or what is shaping it. A worldview can be defined as a set of core beliefs and guides for how we perceive, interpret, judge, and respond to reality. In part 1, I encouraged you to accept three core beliefs: (1) We live in a broken world with fallen people; (2) we were made for shalom; and (3) Christ, the Master Shalom-Maker, desires for His disciples to live as shalom-makers in His world.

It was crucial for me to start a book on forgiveness with these truths because if Disney's happily-ever-afters or an influencer's carefully curated highlight reel is what's shaping your worldview on friendships and romantic relationships, you will be sorely disappointed. You will be shocked when you don't get the dreamy, romantic relationship you long for, or you'll become disgruntled when your friendships aren't hashtag worthy. But if you lean into the core belief that we live in a broken world with fallen people, you will perceive, interpret, and judge offenses as normal human experiences and respond to them as such. You won't be so shocked that you are unwilling to do the hard work of forgiveness. Your biblical worldview will have prepared your heart to accept the truth that in a broken world with fallen people, offense will happen. Understanding and accepting that Christ has called you to live as a shalom-maker in His world compels you to forgive and, when possible, pursue reconciliation.

In this part of the book, to help fortify your resolve to obey His command to forgive, we will return to the third core belief we discussed in part 1: Christ, the Master Shalom-Maker, desires for His disciples to live as shalom-makers in His world. We will look at a crucial moment in Jesus's life where He exhibits forgiveness and observe how His movements in a fallen and broken world are countercultural. We will explore Jesus's teaching on reconciliation, then take a necessary detour to come face-to-face with an unfortunate truth about ourselves. We will conclude this section of the book by bringing everything we've discussed together, laying out a process for forgiveness, and exploring forgiveness as a spiritual discipline.

CHAPTER 8

JESUS, JUDAS, AND CANCEL CULTURE

Love your enemies.

JESUS, MATTHEW 5:44

We were what they call sister-friends. We went to the same church, were part of the same friend group, and genuinely enjoyed each other. To this day, there is no one I laugh with harder. We bore burdens, shared blessings, confessed fears, and often stayed up late wrestling with the mystery of God's calls on our lives. Since I was on staff at our church and the older one in our friendship, our relationship also had a discipleship aspect to it. Every week we would meet with a few other women from our church for accountability, prayer, and time in God's Word. Looking back, I question if it was wise to have so many layers and intersections to our relationship. But I really thought we were faithfully living out the ethos of the Acts 2 church, devoting ourselves to the apostles' teaching, fellowship, meal sharing, prayer, and having one another's back (verses 42-45).

As the relationship turned bitter, I started to feel relationally unsafe and was desperately looking for the exit. But I also felt trapped. Our church was small, so I had no way to avoid her. Plus our friend group was so tight that to pull away from her would also mean to pull away from the group. But, one night, while staring at the ceiling with tears steadily flowing down my face, I told Jesus I was done. I was done faithfully casting forgiven sins back into the depths of the sea as new offenses were made. I was done humbly confronting and was ready to leave, ghost, and cancel. I was done trying to be like Him, decisively committing to His seventy times seven forgiveness expectation. As I told Jesus all the ways I was done, He interrupted my lament and reminded me of His relationship with Judas.

JESUS, JUDAS, AND CANCEL CULTURE

I've always wondered what Jesus's initial encounter with Judas was like. Did Jesus's heart beat faster when He first laid eyes on the man who would betray Him? Did Jesus struggle to call out Judas's name when it was time to set apart the Twelve? Being both fully human and fully divine, surely Jesus knew, well before His hour would come, the role Judas would play in His story. But even still, He called Judas to come in close. For three years, Jesus and Judas lived like a family along with a cohort of other brothers and sisters. Side-by-side they broke bread, shared laughs, survived the hardships of inclement weather, and endured the social persecution of the Pharisees. For thousands upon thousands of miles, Judas followed in the steps of his Rabbi, Jesus. And even though Judas didn't know the uprising pending in his heart, Jesus did. Jesus knew that each step and every mile they walked together was leading them closer to Judas's betrayal. But before Judas sealed his betrayal with a kiss, Jesus washed his feet. The apostle John alerts us to this grand act of mercy, writing:

> During supper, *when the devil had already put it into the heart of Judas Iscariot,* Simon's son, to betray him, Jesus, knowing that the Father had given all things into his hands, and that he had come from God and was going back to God, rose from supper. He laid aside his outer garments,

and taking a towel, tied it around his waist. *Then he poured water into a basin and began to wash the disciples' feet* and to wipe them with the towel that was wrapped around him (John 13:2-5, emphasis mine).

Even though Judas has already betrayed His trust, Jesus still washes Judas's feet. When it's Judas's turn to get his feet washed, Jesus doesn't passive-aggressively skip over him. Instead, Jesus gets down on bended knee, takes on the role of a humble servant, and cleans His betrayer's filthy feet. But Christ's mercy doesn't start or end here. Before He washes Judas's feet, Jesus allows Judas to participate in communion. Then after washing His disciples' feet, Jesus speaks of His coming betrayal by saying, "He who ate my bread has lifted his heel against me" (John 13:18). This bread Jesus is referring to is the same bread He has just blessed, broken, and shared with His disciples, saying, "This is my body, which is given for you" (Luke 22:19).

Jesus, deeply "troubled in his spirit," humbly and mercifully confronts His betrayer by announcing to the group, "Truly, truly, I say to you, one of you will betray me" (John 13:21). Anxious and unsure about whom among them Jesus is speaking, the apostle John asks Him to name His betrayer. Jesus responds, "It is he to whom I will give this morsel of bread when I have dipped it" (John 13:26). Then Jesus dips a piece of bread, representative of His body, into the cup, representative of His blood shed for the forgiveness of sins, and offers communion to Judas *again*. This is beautiful, because though Judas's betrayal would create a direct path to the cross, Jesus assures Judas that He is going to the cross for his sins as well. Jesus died for Judas too. If Judas repented and appealed to the resurrected Savior for forgiveness, I wholeheartedly believe, he would've been forgiven. Why? Because even though Jesus was fully aware of Judas's coming betrayal, Jesus lovingly washed Judas's feet and mercifully offered him communion twice. He never *cancels* him.

CANCEL CULTURE
VERSUS JESUS CULTURE

In 1981, after a disappointing first date, Nile Rodgers of the band Chic wrote "Your Love Is Cancelled." As an avid television watcher, Rodgers used a network's choice to cancel a TV show as an analogy for cancelling or ending a relationship. Though the song didn't gain much traction, the idea did, eventually becoming a colloquialism to describe a relationship's end that found a home in the Black community through film and music. As Clyde McGrady, writer for the *Washington Post*, explains, "Cancellations were more of a personal decision, a way to say we don't really kick it anymore: You stepped out of line and now I'm done with you."[1] But as the personal practice of cancelling went viral, it became a cultural norm, shaping the way people relate to others both privately and publicly—so much so that cancelling, unfollowing, and unfriending someone online or in real life is encouraged and even praised if by doing so you "protect your peace" or "delete toxic people" from your life.

Were Jesus to enter our twenty-first-century narrative, He would call us to repent of cancel culture. He would challenge the cultural mantras that tell us to protect our peace from so-called toxic people. I imagine He would address us, much like He addresses the Jews in Matthew 5 and Luke 6: "You've heard that it's acceptable to cancel those who wrong you. But I say to you: Love your enemies, and do good toward them and lend to them, expecting nothing in return. And if you do, your reward will be great, and you will be sons and daughters of the Most High, who He is kind to the ungrateful and the evil. Be merciful, even as your Father is merciful." Cancel culture is antithetical to the mercy-filled and shalom-making culture Jesus is seeking to create among His disciples.

Almost every time Jesus teaches on forgiveness, He mentions His Kingdom. In the Lord's Prayer, the Kingdom Jesus prays would come is a Kingdom where citizens forgive their debtors as they have been forgiven (Matthew 6:12; Luke 11:4). When Jesus is setting the norms of His Kingdom in His inaugural sermon, He calls for His disciples to "forgive, and you will be forgiven" (Luke 6:37). Before Jesus goes into the parable of the unforgiving servant, He says, "Therefore the kingdom of heaven may be compared" (Matthew 18:23). The Kingdom of heaven is one where those who have generously received mercy extend generous mercy to others. Jesus consistently situates His command to forgive in the reality of His coming and reigning Kingdom. Forgiveness is a cultural Kingdom value norm and is expected to be the ethos and practice of all its forgiven citizens.

However, as my good friend and founder of the Jude 3 Project Lisa V. Fields points out, cancelling and ghosting is the standard, not mercy and forgiveness. While on a part of a panel discussion on how to find peace in a turbulent world, Lisa and her colleagues were asked, "Does having peace with people through forgiveness require reconciliation [to be in a relationship with them again]?" After one panelist quickly responded by saying no, Lisa added this challenge:

> I agree. [Your forgiveness doesn't require reconciliation.] But I would add a challenge to my generation in particular… Sometimes in our cancel culture, we only know how to love till it hurts. We don't know how to love when it hurts…I'm not talking about when it hurts like abuse. [Yes, in those instances, we should not reconcile.] But I'm concerned that my generation doesn't have the discipline of continuing and persevering when relationships hit difficulty. Yes, forgiveness doesn't mean reconciliation, but have you [ever] reconciled with anybody? There are some people you can never reconcile with, but have you ever resolved anything? Or do you just have a trail of broken relationships…do you just cancel people because you have never worked through anything?[2]

Beloved, if you are follower of Jesus Christ and your answer to all of Ms. Fields's questions are no, it's time to cancel your subscription to cancel culture. It's time to denounce the theology of cancel culture that's steeped in defense mechanisms and comfort-seeking and align yourself with the theology of Jesus culture, which is steeped in sacrificial love, mercy, and shalom-making. You will need to trade the beliefs, values, and practices of cancel culture for the beliefs, values, and practices of Jesus culture.

Beliefs

Cancel Culture: People Don't Change. Cancel culture is rooted in a worldview that says people can't change. If we return to Nile Rodgers's TV cancellation analogy, cancel culture treats someone like a plotline in a show that can't be revived or a story that's no longer worth telling. But as image-bearers, every human being, even the "chiefs" among sinners, possesses the ability to change. Their plotline can be revived. Before we cancel and ghost them, we should, like Christ, humbly confront them, giving them an opportunity to repent and relate to us in a more godly way. If given a shot, they may change.

Jesus Culture: Jesus Can Change People. As Christians, we subscribe to the truth that Jesus can change people. We believe Jesus has the power to make us into a new creation. If we can claim this truth for ourselves, why can't we claim it for others? Herein lies the hypocritical pitfall of cancel culture. When we mess up, we want people to hear us out, give us the benefit of the doubt, and love us despite our weaknesses and shortcomings. We long for, and maybe even expect, those we've offended to extend understanding, forgiveness, and grace without hesitation. But when the tables are turned and we are the offended in the narrative, we can be guilty of not doing the same. We forget all the other wonderful characteristics about them and only see them through the lens of their sin; we conclude that the person is only a liar, adulterer, and gossiper who won't change.

But they can. Especially if they've experienced the transformative power of the gospel.

Values

Cancel Culture: Protect Your Peace. I believe this mantra has become the Achilles' heel of our generation. If the relationship becomes hard and no longer serves us, we're done. However, if we're honest, the "protect your peace" philosophy along with the cancel culture mindset has become a kind of new age defense mechanism we can use to protect ourselves. I know I have. But this protective response is steeped in fear, not love. So while earthly wisdom tells us to run as fast as we can when someone sins against us, we need to hold this in tension with the call to make every effort "to maintain the unity of the Spirit in the bond of peace" (Ephesians 4:3). Yes, on occasion we will need to create physical and emotional distance in a relationship. But this should not be our default setting for handling conflict and offense; shalom-making should.

Jesus Culture: God's Children Are Shalom-Makers. As children of God, we are shalom-makers. This is a part of our fundamental identity as Christ followers. Forgiveness and reconciliation, when possible, are nonnegotiable. We serve a forgiving and reconciling God. We have been carved in the image of the Master Shalom-Maker, and mercy and forgiveness are core values of His Kingdom. And how can we not embody these values when, were it not for God's mercy and forgiveness, we would be hell-bound? If God—who had every justification and right to cancel us—chose not to, how much more should we refrain from the practice of cancelling others?

Practices

Cancel Culture: Remove Toxic People from Your Life. While we'll need to end or restructure relationships with so-called toxic people at times, I wonder if our definition of *toxic* is too broad. What if what we've labeled as *toxic* isn't toxic, but just human? What if the person who offended you isn't showing signs of their toxicity, but their humanity? As a finite and fallen human being, they are incapable of getting it right 100 percent of the time. They will mess up. As my friend, pastor, and counselor Dr. Evan Marbury explains, "When we are in relationship with others, whether that be through family, work, church, etc., there will come a time where we hurt one another…But not all hurt is harm."[3]

Beloved, not all offenses should be perceived as toxic or harmful. Remember, in a broken world with fallen people, we will inevitably get hurt. People will fail us—even the ones who know Jesus and eagerly follow Him. We must be able to discern the difference between human and abusive behavior. The two are not the same and require different responses, but, too often, they receive the same response. To help us discern the difference, Dr. Marbury defines abuse as "an exploitive use of power over another for self-interested gains."[4] When we encounter this kind of abuse, we will need to end or restructure the relationship. However, we do not cancel them as someone whose plotline cannot be redeemed. Ending and restructuring, not cancelling, is meant to be a form of accountability.

Jesus Culture: Love Your Enemy. In Matthew 5:39, Jesus tells His disciples to not retaliate against an evil person. Then, in Matthew 5:44, He tells His disciples to love their enemies. I believe Jesus appeals to us to respond this way because an evil person is far from the life of God. Their sin doesn't only make them your enemy; it makes them God's enemy as well. Jesus's call for restraint, love, and forgiveness is a call to be a living, breathing embodiment of the gospel. It's an invitation to proclaim the gospel of Jesus, offering forgiveness and reconciliation to those who repent and believe. Beloved, here is another hard truth you must accept: Jesus is equally invested in your salvation as He is in the salvation of those who have wronged you. He commands us to forgive because every time we do, we put the gospel on grand display. If you forgive your offender, maybe God will forgive them too? If you don't cancel them, maybe God won't either.

ONE LAST THING

Before we move forward, there is one more cultural mantra I must address. In both Christian and non-Christian spaces, we are often encouraged to forgive to free ourselves. While there is truth to this mantra, Jesus's primary encouragement to forgive isn't a promised future; it's a settled past. We are to forgive *because we have been forgiven*. These two encouragements to forgive are drastically different. The call to forgive for personal freedom can be steeped in the same kind of self-conscious, self-centered self-preservation of their offender. It says, "We forgive for our sake, not theirs." But as my pastor Ryan Brooks often reminds me and the good people of Vertical Church, the root words of *forgive* are *for* and *give*. Forgiveness is a *gift for* the other person.

Plus, depending on the person and the situation, forgiveness may not always feel like freedom. For a person who has been cheated on by their spouse, for instance, forgiveness doesn't immediately feel like freedom. It can feel like a prison. In those initial days of shock and making the decision to forgive, the forgiver will have to decisively commit moment-by-moment to faithfully cast their spouse's infidelity into the depths of the sea. Forgiveness will very much look and feel like a *gift for* their spouse's freedom, not themselves. This promise of personal freedom can also be a disappointing mirage for those who have suffered abuse. Though God is healing them, and though their trauma isn't as disruptive as it's been in the past, when they are triggered, they are pulled right into the pain along with its sights, sounds, and smells as if it happened yesterday.

In Christ, we find a better way to go about forgiveness. Sandwiched right in between the acknowledgement that Judas's heart was already set to betray Jesus and Jesus's decision to wash Judas's feet are these words: "Jesus, *knowing* that the Father had given all things into his hands, and that he had come from God and was going back to God, rose from supper" (John 13:3-4, emphasis mine). It is from this place of knowing that Jesus rises to wash the feet of nine men who would desert Him, one who would deny Him three times, and another who would betray Him. Knowing His Father will give Him all things *frees* Him of the need to seek retribution on His own behalf. Knowing that the Father has sent Him into the world to make shalom *frees* Him from the desire to retaliate against Judas and the others in anger. Knowing that the pain of betrayal would be temporary because He is going back into God's presence *frees* Him to forgive. Jesus forgives *from* freedom, not *for* freedom.

Just as it was for Jesus, sandwiched right in between your offender's betrayal and your merciful decision to forgive are the truths that God will give us all things, that He has sent us into the world to make shalom, and that all the pain we endure this side of heaven is temporal (Revelation 21:4). From this place of knowing—this place of safety, security, and shalom in God—we, too, can rise to forgive.

Beloved, we don't forgive *for* freedom; we forgive *from* freedom. We don't forgive to arrive at a place of freedom. We forgive because, in Christ, we already securely reside in the place of freedom.

SELAH: For this selah, let's sit with Jesus's culture-shifting teaching in Matthew 5:43-47 (csb):

> [43] You have heard that it was said, **Love your neighbor** and hate your enemy. [44] But I tell you, love your enemies and pray for those who persecute you, [45] so that you may be children of your Father in heaven. For he causes his sun to rise on the evil and the good, and sends rain on

the righteous and the unrighteous. [46] For if you love those who love you, what reward will you have? Don't even the tax collectors do the same? [47] And if you greet only your brothers and sisters, what are you doing out of the ordinary? Don't even the Gentiles do the same?

READ: Read Matthew 5:43-47 slowly and pause over any words or phrases that stand out to you.

REFLECT: Read Matthew 5:43-47 slowly and pause over verse 45. Meditate on God's enduring love toward the unjust, remembering that all of humanity falls into this category. No one is just but God.

RESPOND: Consider what it looks like for you to respond to the instruction in these verses.

- What's one way you can pray for your enemy?
- Is the Spirit leading you to love your offender in any practical way? If engaging with your offender in any way would create an opportunity for further harm, please stick to loving them through prayer.

REST: Take a moment and pray for your enemy. Rest knowing that God delights in your step of obedience.

CHAPTER 9

FORGIVENESS DOESN'T EQUAL RECONCILIATION

*If he refuses to listen...let him be to
you as a Gentile and a tax collector.*

JESUS, MATTHEW 18:17

fter sharing with my counselor about my sister-friend's betrayal,
she asked me the most unexpected question: "Yana, have you
considered making any changes to the relationship?" My face must
have revealed that I had never considered such a thing, because she
began to share with me a handful of ways I could restructure our
friendship to regain a sense of emotional safety. As she offered some
suggestions, I remember thinking, *Is my* Christian *counselor suggest-
ing that I cancel my friend—my sister in Christ? Is this even biblical?
Would Jesus—the One who forgave and washed Judas's feet—approve of
me willfully choosing to end the relationship?* It all sounded odd and
antithetical to the mercy-filled and shalom-making culture Jesus
sought to create among His disciples.

In all honesty, I didn't consider any of her suggestions. I counted
them as bones to be separated and discarded from the other good
meaty counsel she offered during that session. However, when my
pastor suggested the very same thing a few weeks later, I became

utterly confused. I needed to search the scriptures for clarity. Didn't forgiveness equal reconciliation? If not, how could I know that I had truly forgiven someone? Were there ever any "terms and conditions" for extending forgiveness but withholding reconciliation? If so, how would I determine this distinction?

I know many are wrestling with this question for sincere reasons. We've heard Jesus's command to forgive and love our enemy, and we are trying to discern what it looks like in practice when the person is unsafe. However, some of us are asking this question because we're looking for an exit. Our model of forgiveness is to forgive and cancel, not to forgive and stay long enough to see what's relationally possible—in other words: "I forgive you, but you can stay over there."

At varying points in my life, I have been either the person sincerely wrestling with this question or the person looking for an exit. However, I think what also caused me to wrestle with this question the most was my failure to recognize that *forgiveness* and *reconciliation* are two words with two distinct meanings requiring two different kinds of work. Because I often heard the two taught together, I assumed forgiveness equaled reconciliation. However, in His teaching, Jesus clarifies that this is not the case and lays out the terms and conditions under which reconciliation should or should not follow forgiveness. But before we get to Jesus's teaching, let's take a closer look at the distinct definitions of these two terms.

TERMS AND DEFINITIONS

So far we've defined *forgiveness* as *the merciful decision to release an offender of a debt and not retaliate against them in anger.* It's your personal decision to release your offender from the responsibility to pay you back and abandon any desire to seek revenge. Forgiveness is a solo work you do before God independent of your offender's apology, explanation, or plea for forgiveness. However, where forgiveness is the *solo work* of the offended, reconciliation is the *shared work* of both the offended and the offender.

Reconciliation is *the committed decision of both the offended and the offender to do the hard work of restoring safety, security, and shalom in the relationship.* Reconciliation is not a work you can do alone. Let me say that again for those of you who, like me, have a strong desire for harmony and will try to put the relationship on your back and fix what's broken on your own: Reconciliation is not a work you can do alone. It's *shared work.* When you roll up your sleeves and try to do the shared work of reconciliation solo, you are relationally over-functioning. As author and podcast host of *The Next Right Thing* Emily P. Freeman wisely explains, "Over-functioning doesn't only apply to our work [life]. It can also show up in our relationships; for example, being overly responsible for outcomes or over attentive to someone else's emotional well being."[1] When you attempt to do the work of reconciliation alone, you become "overly responsible" for the restorative outcomes of the relationship. Instead of holding your offender accountable for their actions, you take responsibility for them by doing one or all of the following:

- You tell yourself you shouldn't have said or done this or that. It's your fault that the other person is angry, and you need to be more mindful of their mood, trauma, expectations, and triggers next time.

- You take on the responsibility of fixing them. If you just hold space for them and love them unconditionally, maybe they will change. But, friend, you are neither their therapist nor their savior.

- To restore shalom, you rush in and apologize even though you have done nothing wrong.

- Your God-given empathy causes you to make concessions

for their behavior or their emotional and spiritual immaturity. You figure you should give them a pass because they
had a bad day or are still deeply wounded by their past.

Though there are times to extend this form of kindness and understanding to others, when this becomes the norm of the relationship,
you are over-functioning. You are doing more than what is good and
right for you and them. By taking on the responsibility to restore relational harmony, you enable their behavior. But what is good, right,
and needed for the relationship to live beyond offense is humble
confrontation and a call for repentance. Without these steps, you
may succeed at keeping the peace, but you will fall short of making
shalom. For true reconciliation to be achieved, you need to discern
where your work begins and ends, then do no more or less.

TERMS AND CONDITIONS

Thankfully Jesus doesn't leave us in the dark about where our work in
the reconciliation process ends and where our offender's work begins.
He also doesn't shame us for asking the question: Does forgiveness
always equal reconciliation? In fact, He anticipates the question and
provides us with a clear, practical, and compelling answer. In both
the message of the gospel and in His teachings, He clearly lays out
the terms and conditions for when to move beyond an offense and
do the hard-yet-worthy work of reconciliation.

In the Message of the Gospel

At the cross Jesus does the solo work of providing forgiveness for
the past, present, and future sins of the entire human race. In 1 John
2:2, the apostle John writes, "[Jesus] himself is the atoning sacrifice
for our sins, and not only for ours, but also for those of the whole
world" (csb). Though John is writing to a Christian audience, he

clarifies for them that Jesus didn't just die for the sins of believers; He died for *everyone's* sin. Apart from receiving an apology or retribution, Jesus willfully dies for us all. From a place of safety, security, and shalom in His relationship with God, He freely humbles Himself "by becoming obedient to the point of death, even death on a cross" (Philippians 2:8). While we were yet sinners, Christ died (Romans 5:6). Before we turned to Him with repentance and faith, Christ made the merciful decision to release us of our sin debt and not retaliate against us. He forgave us willingly, freely, and fully. No terms or conditions predicated His forgiveness. It was a solo work He did to please the Father.

However, there are terms and conditions that must be met to experience Jesus's gift of forgiveness and be reconciled to Him. We must respond to Jesus's call to "repent and believe in the gospel" (Mark 1:15). We must, by faith, claim Jesus's atoning work on the cross as the only means by which our relationship with God can be restored. We must repent by transferring our allegiance from the kingdom of darkness to the Kingdom of heaven. Those are the terms and conditions for experiencing the gift of God's forgiveness and being reconciled to Him. In John 1:12, the apostle John writes, "To all who did receive him, who believed in his name, he gave the right to become children of God."

Here's the guiding principle on forgiveness and reconciliation we receive from the message of the gospel: *Forgiveness is for everybody; reconciliation is for a repentant few.* Through the message of the gospel Jesus says to us, "Beloved, even if they never apologize, join Me in willingly, freely, and fully forgiving them. They may stiff-arm your forgiveness, but don't stiffen your arm against My call to extend mercy and grace. Even if they sin against you 77 times, with your eyes fixed on Me and My death for your never-ending list of sins, forgive. Draw your inspiration and strength from My tattered body, hung on the cross for the forgiveness of your sins."

Once again, we encounter my favorite thing about Jesus. He never asks us to do something He hasn't already done. He always goes first, setting the tone and providing us with inspiration and the blueprint for how to respond to offense. Confession, repentance, and faith in Him are necessary for reconciling one's relationship with Him. Without these, reconciliation is not possible, and the relational distance remains. Forgiveness is for everybody; reconciliation is for a repentant few. If these are Jesus's terms and conditions for reconciliation, how much more should and can they be ours?

In His Teachings

We not only find the principle—forgiveness is for everybody; reconciliation is for the repentant few—in the message of the gospel; we also find it clearly spelled out in Jesus's teachings. In Matthew 18:15-20, Jesus shares these words with His disciples:

> If your brother sins against you, go tell him his fault, between you and him alone. If he listens to you, you have won your brother. But if he won't listen, take one or two others with you, so that by the testimony of two or three witnesses every fact may be established. If he doesn't pay attention to them, tell the church. If he doesn't pay attention even to the church, let him be like a Gentile and a tax collector to you. Truly I tell you, whatever you bind on earth will have been bound in heaven, and whatever you loose on earth will have been loosed in heaven. Again, truly I tell you, if two of you on earth agree about any matter that you pray for, it will be done for you by my Father in heaven. For where two or three are gathered together in my name, I am there among them (csb).

Reconciliation Flow Chart
Matthew 18:15-20

Forgive → Go and tell your offender their faults → Did they listen? → Yes / No

Yes → Rejoice + Reconcile

No → Invite two trustworthy others for mediation and accountability → Did they listen? → Yes / No

Yes → Rejoice + Reconcile

No → Invite the Christ-following community for mediation and accountability → Did they listen? → Yes / No

Yes → Rejoice + Reconcile

No → Restructure or End the Relationship

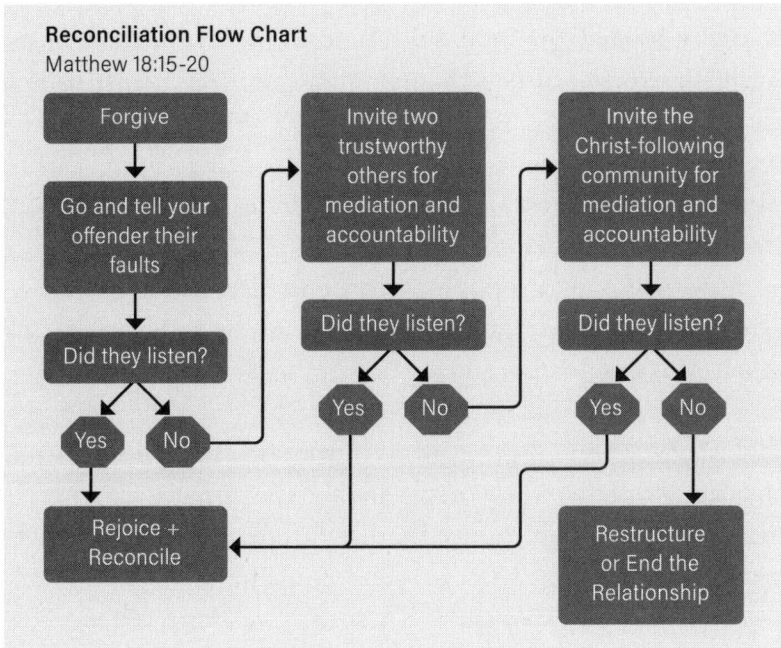

Let's walk through the terms and conditions we are called to follow when trying to discern if we should reconcile with an offender.

IF THEY LISTEN, THEN RECONCILE

The first term Jesus establishes for reconciliation is listening. In the scriptures, listening is more than merely hearing what another person has said; it is *agreeing* and *believing* that what has been said is true by *responding* or *repenting* accordingly.[2] As it is with the message of the gospel, reconciliation is only possible when confession and repentance are present.

Confession is an admittance of wrong that agrees with God's definition of right and wrong—not your own. When you humbly confront a person about their sin against you, your offense must find its credibility in God's Word, not your preferences or expectations.

You must be able to discern if their offense is truly the result of sin or the by-product of forgetfulness, miscommunication, or personality differences. However, because it is not always easy to discern if our offense is warranted, Jesus advises us to bring in two or more witnesses to help determine if the complaint is justifiable. The judicial language is intentional.

As witnesses, their role is to verify or dismiss the claim you have against your offender. If a consensus still can't be met, you need to solicit the counsel of the church—the Christ-following community—to decipher who's truly in the wrong. Maybe it's not the other person. Maybe it's you. But regardless of who is at fault, if the two of you, along with the two witnesses and the Christ-following community, can't agree or confess together that the offense is founded, reconciliation isn't possible. I hate to sound churchy, but: "Can two walk together, except they be agreed?" (Amos 3:3 KJV). Sure, you may continue to do life with each other, but there may always be a wedge of distrust between you. Your physical proximity may not change, but your relational and emotional proximity inevitably will. Agreement and confession are paramount if reconciliation is to be achieved, but they only satisfy half of Jesus's definition of listening. The confession needs to be followed with repentance. If not, the confession is no more than an empty apology.

Repentance is turning away from a behavior or way of thinking that is oppositional to God and His ways, then bringing those thoughts and behaviors into alignment with Him. Again, the emphasis is on God and His ways, not our own. When our calls for repentance don't find their credibility in what God desires, we are likely demanding or requiring more from others than what God requires. But when they are aligned, we have the blessed assurance of knowing we are asking them to live up to God's standards, not ours. And herein lies the bigger picture you and I need to keep in mind when someone sins against us: Their sin is not only offensive to us; it is also offensive to

God. So when you go to them privately to humbly confront their sin against you, you are not only making an appeal for them to be reconciled to you. You are also, and more importantly, appealing for them to be reconciled to God. This is why Jesus says, "If [your offender] listens to you, you have gained your brother [or sister]" (Matthew 18:15). If they don't, you have lost them. If they are lost to you, they are likely in some way also lost and adrift from God. And this is true even if they are a Christian. For this reason, Jesus compels you and me to go and seek the help of two mediating witnesses and the Christ-following community if necessary.

Our offender's lack of relational alignment with us reveals a lack of relational alignment with God. But if they confess and show signs of repentance, it reveals they are ready to roll up their sleeves and do the hard work of living beyond offense with you. In response to their confession and repentance, Jesus calls us to get into the dirt with them, to uproot the weeds of distrust, and learn to trust them again. However, their repentance may not be an immediate and complete 180. It will likely be slower and more incremental than you would like. But if their repentance is measurable and sincere, Jesus commands us to pursue reconciliation, to enter and endure the awkwardness or discomfort of learning to trust and enjoy them again. However, the pace and degree of their repentance should dictate the pace and degree of your trust. You'll find more on what it looks like to trust an offender again in part 5 of this book.

IF THEY DON'T LISTEN, RESTRUCTURE OR END THE RELATIONSHIP

If their confession and repentance are completely lacking, Jesus calls for a relational shift. He says, "If [your offender] refuses to listen even to the church, let [them] be to you as a Gentile and a tax collector" (Matthew 18:17). If Jesus's command seems odd, and even a bit severe, that's a fair response. But when Jesus says, "Let [them] be to you as a Gentile or tax collector," He is not being derogatory or exclusive. He's also not making an allowance for you to cancel them. He is, once again, using his audience's historical, cultural, and social context to describe how they are to relate to their unrepentant offender moving forward.

Jesus's command to treat your unrepentant offender as a Gentile is a call for you to redefine the relationship. Because of their refusal to confess and repent of their wrongdoing, you no longer must relate to them as a brother or sister in Christ but instead as an unbelieving Gentile. Where you once shared all things in common, you now withhold that kind of generosity until the person repents. Where you once bore burdens, push pause on offering that kind of emotional support until the person recognizes and confesses how their sin has become a burden for you. You can be generous and empathetic. You are still called to love them, but you should adjust your expectations and approach (Matthew 5:43-48). They are no longer behaving as a sibling invested in your mutual well-being, but as an enemy more committed to their own. Their refusal to listen proves they have deviated from the ethics of Jesus's Kingdom and will more than likely reoffend, causing even greater hurt or harm. In these unfortunate cases, you need to adjust your boundaries and relational rhythms.

Again, Jesus's call to break fellowship with your unrepentant offender is a call to make an appeal on God's behalf for them to repent and be reconciled to God. You are not withholding and withdrawing from the relationship for your personal peace, but for their eternal shalom. By regarding them as an unbelieving Gentile, your primary concern is their misalignment with God. Your withholding and withdrawing are acts of humble confrontation. It's your way of turning the other cheek in hopes that your offender would wake up from their sin and repent, turning to God and His ways.

Depending on the relationship, circumstances, and offense, this break in fellowship could be full or partial. You may not need to end the relationship but only restructure it. For example, because they have shown themselves to be untrustworthy or manipulative with money, you now refrain from loaning money or asking for it. They may still be able to come to a cookout, and you might not need to leave your small group, but because they tend to be unkind with their words, you no longer extend invitations to intimate gatherings and meals. You limit their access to you emotionally, and when necessary, physically.

In Jesus's context, tax collectors were regarded as traitors and thieves not to be trusted. This was especially true if they were Jewish. Instead of standing in solidarity with their people under the oppression of Rome, tax collectors of Jewish descent partnered with Rome to get a leg up in the world. As an act of self-conscious, self-centered self-preservation, they overtaxed the Jews for financial gain and social status. In light of their oppressive nine-to-five, tax collectors were "generally avoid[ed] since even to be seen by them might invite their abuse. The rabbis compared encountering a tax collector to meeting up with an angry bear. Such an encounter never ended well."[3] So when Jesus instructs us to regard an unrepentant offender as a tax collector, He isn't speaking derogatorily. He's expressing concern for our safety. Like an angry bear, an unrepentant offender is unsafe. To live near them will only incite further abuse—physically, emotionally, or psychologically.

Beloved, Jesus calls you to forgive, but He does not call you to reconcile with an abusive person. He cares deeply about your safety and your shalom. In His love for you, He instructs you to end your relationship with those who deny the truth, blame-shift, gaslight, manipulate, or abuse you. You are instructed not only to limit their access to you but also to cut it off entirely until they confess their sin and show significant signs of repentance. But even then, proceed with much caution and in partnership with the counsel of trusted others.

DON'T MAKE THE DECISION
TO RECONCILE, WITHHOLD,
OR WITHDRAW ALONE

Though Jesus's teaching on reconciliation is straightforward, we often don't follow the flowchart presented earlier in the chapter. We can either hang on to the relationship for too long because the pain of bringing it to an end seems more unbearable than the pain of staying in it, or we can let go of it too soon because we anxiously feel the need to protect our well-being. When we do the latter, our modus operandi is to skip Jesus's instruction to confront the offender privately and instead vent and gossip to a friend. Even if we do confront the offender privately, our pursuit of reconciliation ends there. We don't reach to others for help. But if we do reach out to two witnesses, it isn't for help resolving the issue. No, we're just calling to let them know we're done, that we've had enough, and that our offender is cancelled. We just want someone else to validate our feelings and conclusions, not challenge them. I know all this because the "we" in these sentences is me. However, as I've meditated and applied Jesus's teaching on reconciliation, I have come to understand the brilliance of Jesus's instruction.

When we are hurt and in the thick of conflict with someone we love, we are not always good judges. We need to bring in others to ensure we are seeing things clearly. We need the two witnesses to help us discern whether our complaint is justified. We need the Christ-following community to help us discern whether reconciliation is possible and, if not, how to move forward. To guard us from hastily restructuring or ending relationships with those who've hurt or harmed us, Jesus wisely puts these terms and conditions in place for us to follow. And these principles can still apply when our grievances are with a person who doesn't know Jesus. The conversation will no doubt look different, but as followers of Jesus we are still called to humbly confront those who offend us. Remember, the issue at hand is bigger than their sin against us. They have also sinned against God.

While bringing in someone from church to mediate a conflict with an unbelieving family member or coworker may be unwise, you can bring in a counselor, wise auntie, or objective coworker. Even when your offender is a Christian but goes to another church, you can use these terms and conditions for reconciliation. It might be inappropriate for you to bring in your pastor or small group Bible study leader to mediate. But if the two of you are a part of Christ-following friend group, you can and should invite the group in to mediate and provide counsel on if and how the relationship can move forward.

REST IN THE COUNSEL OF THE CHRIST-FOLLOWING COMMUNITY

So do you have recourse when forgiving is possible but reconciliation is not? Yes, but, in some cases it will and should be difficult. You love them and you don't want to lose them. You long for shalom and can't imagine that Jesus would want you to let the relationship go. Knowing how reluctant we might be to restructure or end a relationship with someone we love, Jesus adds these reassuring words:

> Truly I tell you, whatever you bind on earth will have been bound in heaven, and whatever you loose on earth will have been loosed in heaven. Again, truly I tell you, if two of you on earth agree about any matter that you pray for, it will be done for you by my Father in heaven. For where two or three are gathered together in my name, I am there among them (verses 18-20 CSB).

Jesus knows ending a relationship with someone you love and once trusted hurts. He knows that under certain circumstances, we will not want to part ways with a spouse we vowed never to leave or forsake apart from death, or with a family member whose love we've always longed for. He's aware that we will talk ourselves into going back to the relationship even after—in agreement with our Christ-following community, counselor, and auntie—we have decided to leave. He knows we tend to misread, misinterpret, and misapply His commands to love our enemy and turn the other cheek. But "love your enemy" doesn't mean cuddle up with them, and "turn the other cheek" doesn't mean sticking beside them no matter what. If they don't listen, Jesus commands relational and physical distance. In His closing statements to His teaching on reconciliation, He says, "If your offender will not listen, and if the judgment of the Christ-following community is to end the relationship, I'm with you. Whatever the Christ-following community decides, I will back you."

In time, I came to follow my counselor's and pastor's suggestions. It was hard, and I often questioned whether I made the right decision, but Jesus's closing statement to His teaching on reconciliation brought me so much comfort. Whenever I doubt my decision, I am assured that I did because I didn't make it alone. Under the counsel of my counselor and Christ-following community, I set boundaries and accepted the relationship's necessary end. It was and still is painful. But my conscience is clear. I am assured that what has been collectively decided by the Christ-following community here on earth is affirmed by Christ in heaven. However, I still wait, in hope, that my sister-friend and I will find an alternate ending to our story. I pray that God would be so gracious to us that we will laugh as hard as we did when our friendship first began.

SELAH: For this selah, let's read Jesus's teaching on reconciliation again in Matthew 18:15-20:

> [15] If your brother sins against you, go and tell him his fault, between you and him alone. If he listens to you, you have

gained your brother. [16] But if he does not listen, take one or two others along with you, that every charge may be established by the evidence of two or three witnesses. [17] If he refuses to listen to them, tell it to the church. And if he refuses to listen even to the church, let him be to you as a Gentile and a tax collector. [18] Truly, I say to you, whatever you bind on earth shall be bound in heaven, and whatever you loose on earth shall be loosed in heaven. [19] Again I say to you, if two of you agree on earth about anything they ask, it will be done for them by my Father in heaven. [20] For where two or three are gathered in my name, there am I among them.

READ: Read Matthew 18:15-20 slowly and pause over any words or phrases that stand out to you.

REFLECT: Read Matthew 18:15-20 slowly again. Consider the wisdom in Jesus's teaching and how it might have been helpful in past relationships that have ended or in current ones that might need to.

RESPOND: Review the flowchart in this chapter and consider how you might need to use it.

- What ought to be your first or next step in applying Jesus's teaching?

- Who in your Christ-following community, family, or friend group do you think could be potential mediators for you in this conflict or when other conflicts arise?

REST: Read verses 18-20 slowly again. Rest in Jesus's promise to bind and loose in heaven what's bound and loosed by the Christ-following community.

CHAPTER 10

THE UNFORTUNATE TRUTH

What causes quarrels and what causes fights among you?
Is it not this, that your passions are at war within you?

JAMES, JAMES 4:1

I yelled. I raised my voice. Sure, I was mad and thought my friend's expectations were unreasonable. But yelling? That was unacceptable. It was also unexpected.

If you poll those closest to me, they would say I'm gentle, careful with my words, and ever mindful of my tone. When I get mad, I usually shut down, not buck up. But in this moment, I was so fed up with yet another complaint that I let my anger fly. For months I had been holding in feelings of being underappreciated and held to a standard that was not being reciprocated. To maintain my innocence against accusations that I was being an inattentive friend, I put aside my gentle tone and picked up an irritated "I've had it up to here" one.

When we got off the phone, I was immediately filled with embarrassment, regret, and guilt. *Did I just yell at a fully grown person? How did I lose such control of my words and my tone?* Better question: *Why couldn't I stop?* I knew I was wrong, but I just kept going. I threw caution and the future of the relationship to the wind. Was it really that big of a deal? Why was I so offended that I felt the need to yell? What was going on inside of me that caused *that* to come outside of me?

James 4:1-3 offers some insight:

> What causes quarrels and what causes fights among you? Is it not this, that your passions are at war within you? You desire and do not have, so you murder. You covet and cannot obtain, so you fight and quarrel. You do not have, because you do not ask. You ask and do not receive, because you ask wrongly, to spend it on your passions.

So far I've written this book under the assumption that you, the reader, are offended because someone sinned against you. In this chapter, I want to challenge this assumption because here's the unfortunate truth: Sometimes you're the problem. Now, it may be that at the end of the chapter you still conclude that the cause of the quarrels and fights among you and your offender is their blatant and undeniable sin against you and God. However, you might end up realizing that the cause of your offense is the "passions" at war within you, or you might discover that it's a mix of both. As Pastor John Bevere writes in *The Bait of Satan: Living Free from the Deadly Trap of Offense*: "No matter what the scenario is, we can divide all offended people into two major categories: (1) those who have been treated unjustly and (2) those who *believe* they have been treated unjustly."[1] To help you discern which category your offense falls in, let's answer a question: What is an offense?

WHAT IS AN OFFENSE?

Some offenses break God's moral law, while other offenses break our personal law. There are things we can take offense to because they deviate from God's definition of what is good, right, and wrong, and there are things we can take offense to because they stray from *our* definition of what is good, right, and wrong. When doing the work of forgiveness, and to help us discern how to move forward, we need to be able to determine when someone has broken God's standard or merely broken ours.

God's Law

Though God's definition of what is good, right, and wrong can be found in every page of our Bibles, He has summarized His standards in the Ten Commandments. However, the Ten Commandments have become something many Christians consider remedial. If you grew up in church, you probably haven't read or thought about them since your days in Sunday school. You've graduated from them. You've evolved so much in your walk with God that you think you no longer need them. You can identify an offense on your own. If you didn't grow up in church, you may find the Ten Commandments to be a rigid and stifling list of don'ts. You may ask, "If we are saved by grace through faith, why do I need to memorize or be intimately acquainted with these ten commands?" I get it.

However, the Ten Commandments aren't meant to be a list of rigid, stifling don'ts. They are meant to be a guide for how to make shalom in a broken world with fallen people and your fallen self. They are foundational, not remedial. They are the underpinnings that healthy relationships with God and others are built upon. Let's review them together.

THE TEN COMMANDMENTS

1. Don't have any other gods before the God who created and rescued you.

2. Don't make idols for yourselves.

3. Don't take the Lord's name in vain (meaning, don't drag God's name through the mud by the way you speak or live).

4. Keep the Sabbath day holy by ceasing from all your labor to rest.

5. Honor your father and mother.

6. Do not murder.

7. Do not commit adultery.

8. Do not steal.

9. Do not lie about your neighbor.

10. Do not be jealous or envious of what your neighbor has.

Though these are written as rules to follow, they also act as a guide for lovingly holding others accountable. After God gave Israel these commands, He gave them detailed instructions for how to respond if one of them was broken. If someone devised a plan to kill someone else, they were judged more harshly than someone who did so by accident. If the murder was premeditated, the murderer was to be put to death. But if it was an accident, they were allowed to flee and take refuge in another town (Exodus 21:12-14). Impact wasn't the only determining factor for judgment. Intent and motive were also taken into consideration. If two men were carelessly fighting in the vicinity of a pregnant woman and she got hit and went into premature labor, there were consequences. If the baby was unharmed, only a fine was to be paid. But if the baby was harmed, the payment was "life for life, eye for eye, tooth for tooth, hand for hand, foot for foot, burn for burn, wound for wound, stripe for stripe" (Exodus 21:23-25). The person who carelessly hit the pregnant woman was clearly in the wrong, but the retribution was to be equal to the offense committed. Retribution should balance the scales, not tip them in either a shalom-avoidant or shalom-demanding direction.

HOW TO RESPOND TO OFFENSE

Though the ways God called Israel to respond to offenses don't apply to us today, these examples do provide us with three valuable principles for how to respond to offense:

1. Not all offenses should be responded to in the same way.

While this may seem like common sense, as a high-feeler with an all-or-nothing personality, I need this principle to be clearly stated. When our emotions are high and our sense of shalom is fragile, we can overreact. What should be swept under the rug gets brought up at the dinner table. Offenses that should be given a fair shot at resolution in a counseling office get taken to a lawyer's office. Yes, your offender is getting on yo' very last nerve. Yes, they need to grow up and stop doing the non-sinful annoying thing they said they would. But does their immaturity, forgetfulness, or type B or A personality warrant divorce?

At some point with my dad, I had to accept that his alcoholism and neglect did not spring from a lack of love for me, but from a lack of love for himself. Though the impact of his absence was hurtful, his intent was not to be harmful. Every time he got sober, he called. Every time I had an emergency visit to the hospital, he was the first one there. For longer than I should've, I cast him solely as the villain in my story when he was merely a weary traveler wrestling with an addiction that was suffocating his ability to love God and others well. I had a right to be mad. But eventually, I had to admit my anger was disproportionate to his offense.

Beloved, though we don't have a play-by-play in Scripture for responding to one offense versus another, we need to be mindful that not all offenses warrant the same response. There are everyday missteps and unintentional but impactful offenses, and then there are sinful, category-five offenses that don't just hurt your feelings but change your life. These require different responses, and we must be measured in our response so we don't over- or underreact.

2. There are godly and ungodly ways to respond to an offense.

As mentioned earlier, God institutes guidelines for how to respond to offense to prevent people from seeking more retribution than what was warranted. He knew people were liable to respond to an offense in ungodly ways, so He put the law of retribution in place to keep Israel's warranted emotions and valid pain from swaying them toward becoming shalom-demanding.

Beloved, when someone sins against you, you are responsible for how you respond. There will be no "they made me do it" arguments in heaven. You will have to decide if you will partner with the shalom-making Kingdom of Jesus or the shalom-demanding kingdom of Satan. Will you bravely and lovingly speak up to humbly confront, or will you cancel the offender and be shalom-avoidant? Will you seek shalom or further its unraveling? You didn't get to choose what happened, but you do get to choose what happens next.

3. There is only one Lawgiver and Judge.

God is the One who gives the law, and as the Lawgiver, He is the Judge. He didn't give the children of Israel the Ten Commandments and then leave them to decide how to execute them or mitigate cases. He put guardrails in place for how to hold lawbreakers accountable to His commands. He provided instruction on how to respond when someone trespassed His law. The same is true in the new covenant: Jesus puts His Kingdom ethic in place and provides us with instructions on how to respond to offenders. It's His Kingdom, and He is our King. It's His law, and He is its Judge. To help those who are quarreling remember this truth and put unnecessary fighting to rest, James writes:

> Do not speak evil against one another, brothers. The one who speaks against a brother or judges his brother, speaks evil against the law and judges the law. But if you judge the law, you are not a doer of the law but a judge. There is only one lawgiver and judge, he who is able to save and to destroy. But who are you to judge your neighbor? (James 4:11-12).

As citizens in Christ's Kingdom, our rightful position is under the law alongside our fellow servants, not above it where Christ is seated. He alone is the Lawgiver and the Judge. We have no right to judge (punish) His citizens. It's also not our role to create laws for His citizens to live by.

OUR LAW

Like Pharisees, we have all added to the law, creating unreasonable and heavy yokes for others to bear. In our pride, we instate new universal laws for others to live by. But we didn't create them. They are our "fellow servant," not our servants. Yet, we have appointed ourselves as kings and queens, making addendums to the Ten Commandments and Jesus's teaching, demanding that people live not only by His standards but also by ours.

I can say this so boldly because these are all sins I've committed. I have added to the list of God's commands and responded in ungodly ways when others break my commands. I have put myself in the place of being someone's righteous judge, as if I'm not as sinful and fallen as them. Here are some examples of how our convictions, values, cultural backgrounds, personality preferences, or idols can lead us to create commands for our "fellow servants" to live by.

Our Convictions

Convictions are personal beliefs that inform our sense of right and wrong. Though they may be rooted in God's Word, they can also be rooted in our familial and cultural backgrounds, past positive and negative experiences, pet peeves, and preferences. For example, my parents instilled in me that it is wrong to walk on people's grass or park in front of a stranger's home. These "offenses" aren't morally wrong, but when someone walks on my poorly manicured grass or parks in front of my home, I become immediately offended. My sense of what's right and what's wrong is disrupted, and what should be no more than a mild annoyance becomes a matter of injustice.

Our interpretation of what is just or unjust is attached to our sense of what's right and wrong. However, we must be mindful when this is rooted in something other than God's Word. Our convictions about timeliness, the proper way to load the dishwasher, and where to park the car are not matters of injustice. We can be annoyed, but we need to leave space for others to have different views on the aspects of everyday life. Maybe a person was late because they were taught to be present where they are and, in doing so, they lost track of time. Sure, someone may not load the dishwasher like you do, but are the dishes clean or nah? The house is yours, but the street is the public's. Don't make inconveniences or mere differences in how something trivial *should* work capital relational offenses.

Our Values

Values are principles that shape our approach to our care of self, relationships, and work. Though values can be shared, they are not universal. They can vary from person to person, family to family, church to church, and friend group to friend group. But because they are often fixed in a person's or group's worldview, values can give rise to offense when they are intentionally or unintentionally crossed.

As I tried to make sense of why I yelled at my friend, I realized the source of our quarreling was my value for reciprocity in friendships. I rock heavy with Jesus's command to do unto others as you would have them do unto you, and this relationship, in my opinion, wasn't meeting this standard (Luke 6:31). While I had good reason to be upset, my yelling was uncalled for and revealed my inordinate value for reciprocity. Plus, I was holding on so tightly to Jesus's command to do unto to others as they do unto you that I forgot the command was given to me to obey it, not enforce it.

Anytime our values lead us to sin against others, they're inordinate.[2] Though our values maybe good and well-founded, when they are crossed, we must be careful to not treat these offenses as sinful. My friend's failure to meet my expectation of *felt* reciprocity was not a sinful offense. Maybe a lack of awareness, but not necessarily sinful. And in a lot of ways, it didn't warrant forgiveness. What was warranted was an honest conversation about our unspoken friendship expectations.

Beloved, in our most intimate relationships, we need to make our values and relational expectations known. You should not assume that because the two of you get along and have a lot of fun that your values and expectations are shared. And if you learn they are not, adjust relational expectations accordingly and accept the relationship for what it can be. If you share affinities but not values, enjoy the affinities. Let that person be your concertgoing or workout buddy, but be careful not to hold them to the expectations of a best friend. Whether they are trivial or meaningful, it is unrealistic and unfair to hold someone accountable for values they don't share, and this expectation will inevitably give way to offense. Instead of trying to force that person into being someone they are not, trust God to help you find like-minded people.

While values aren't to be held with the same regard as sinful offenses, in relationships where values are stated and shared, offense may be warranted. When our stated and shared values are crossed, we should bring our grievance to our friend and ask questions. We should state our hurt feelings and express our concern for their change in character. And depending on the importance and weight of the value, we will need to humbly confront and engage in the work of forgiveness and reconciliation when possible. But in doing so, we should be careful not to become their lawgiver and judge.

Our Cultural Backgrounds

In any culture, sinful beliefs, values, and norms need to be abandoned—but most cultural beliefs, values, and norms are inherently neutral. They aren't right or wrong. They're just different. While some people of color find it offensive to put raisins in potato salad, it's not sinful. Questionable, but not sinful. However, raisins are easily forgivable, while other cultural non-sinful offenses are not. But if we are going to embark on the beautiful and rewarding journey of doing life with those of different cultural backgrounds, we need to prepare ourselves to do the work of giving and asking for forgiveness.

Many years ago, after a few weeks of attending my friend, and author of *The Reason for Church*, Brad Edwards's small group, he pulled me aside and said, "Yana, I have never really been in a close relationship with a Black person, and I am painfully aware that I am going to do something to offend you. I don't want to, but I know I will. When I do, will you let me know?" Brad's humility not only made me feel safe, but it also taught me that when doing life with people who are culturally different from me, offense will happen. Not only are we both imperfect, but we've been conditioned to see and move in the world differently. Our convictions and values were shaped in different contexts, making it a higher probability that they will offend me, and I, them.

Brad did indeed unintentionally offend me. It was innocent, but I knew if I held it in, bitterness and distance would grow. I also knew that if he did it again, I would split. But, we had made a pact. When he offended me, I agreed to tell him. So I did, and Brad listened. He didn't brush me off as being too sensitive or seek to defend himself. Instead, he thanked me for letting him know and sincerely apologized. He even had enough humility to not say "it won't happen again." Instead, he doubled down on our previous agreement and asked me to let him know the next time it happened.

Offense will happen—especially in relationships with those culturally different from us. But what makes or breaks a relationship is what happens next. Will you humbly confront and forgive or pridefully judge and cancel? Will they humbly confess and make strides to repent or brush you off and not listen? The future of the relationship depends on what happens next.

Our Personality Preferences

On the Myers-Briggs personality assessment, I register as an ISFJ—an introverted and observing person who feels things deeply and orders their life around a fixed set of judgments. I need time alone. I have a strong sense of what's right and wrong. I'm empathetic and sensitive. I like plans and being on time to make sure I don't miss anything. This is the way God has fearfully and wonderfully made me. However, when I encounter an ENTP—an extroverted and intuitive person who thinks deeply and lives spontaneously—I forget this is how God has fearfully and wonderfully made them. When doing life with people whose personalities are different from ours, we need to respect and love who they are. Instead of demanding them to think and behave like us, we need to accept, and maybe even rejoice in, how God made them. Instead of allowing our personality differences to be the primary cause for quarreling, we need to treat them like opportunities to learn from one another. Clashes over personality differences aren't the places where we need to do the work of forgiveness. They are the places where we need to do the work of patience, gentleness, understanding, and forbearing love.

Our Idols

Anytime we attach one of our idols to a person, conflict is bound to happen. If the people in our lives don't bow down and worship our idols of comfort, respect, preferred love languages, need for certainty, autonomy, perfectionism, and even our love for fun, we will become overly disappointed, take issue with their failure to worship our idols, and charge them with committing a capital offense.

Quarreling and fights will also arise when the people in our lives stifle our ability to worship our idols. If work, entertainment, or finishing your to-do list are your idols, when your roommate, spouse, or child interrupts you with a request, you will huff and puff. You'll say they're the problem and the ones who need to change, but the truth is, you're the problem. Your lack of patience and a servant's heart is the source of the quarrel, not them. Your idolatry is producing the strain in the relationship, not their need. Quarreling can even arise when the imperfections in the relationship expose imperfections in you, shattering the image you've carefully constructed of yourself so that others revere you in a certain way.

After I yelled, I went on a walk. I needed to process what just happened and invite the Lord to inspect my heart. I needed to ask Him why I yelled instead of trying to figure it out by myself. As I walked and talked, He talked back, revealing to me that I didn't just yell at my friend because of my value for reciprocity. I yelled at her because her complaint shattered my image of being an ideal friend. It also exposed my idolatry to friendship and unsettled the parts of me that fears if I don't measure up to people's expectations that they will leave. She wasn't the problem. I was.

Beloved, sometimes, it's you. Sometimes your idolatry is causing the strife in your relationships. When doing the work of forgiveness, we must carefully discern if someone has broken God's law or our personal one and respond accordingly. We need to selah—to pause and ask God to search our heart to reveal if any sin within us is causing the conflict. Only after removing the plank from our eye will we be able to properly remove the speck from our offender's. However, in inviting God to search our heart, we might discover this unfortunate truth: It's us, not them.

SELAH: For this selah, I want to share with you the verses from Psalm 139:23-24 I prayed on my walk:

> [23] Search me, O God, and know my heart!
>   Try me and know my thoughts!
> [24] And see if there be any grievous way in me,
>   and lead me in the way everlasting!

READ: Read Psalm 139:23-24 slowly and pause over any words or phrases that stand out to you.

REFLECT: Read Psalm 139:23-24 slowly again. Invite God to search and inspect your heart. Honestly share with Him the offenses on your heart. Create space for Him to reveal to you if your offenses are warranted.

RESPOND: Read Psalm 139:23-24 again. Invite God to reveal any grievous, sinful, or idolatrous ways in your heart.

- Does this offense expose any idolatry in your heart? If so, does it expose an idol of comfort, certainty, respect, autonomy, perfectionism, or something else?

- Do you need to ask someone for forgiveness? If so, who and for what? Write it out.

REST: Read Psalm 139:23-24 slowly again and pause over the last line. Ask God to lead you in His everlasting way. Invite Him to reveal your next step to honoring Him in your relationships with others. Then commit to do it, and rest.

CHAPTER 11

FORGIVENESS AS A SPIRITUAL DISCIPLINE

Forgive us our debts,
as we also have forgiven our debtors.
JESUS, MATTHEW 6:12

We Westerners really like to make lists and put things into tidy categories. And we especially like to do this when it comes to our faith. We've systematized a theology about God and His world that was passed down to us in story form. We've codified Jesus's command to "follow Me" into a list of spiritual disciplines. Don't get me wrong; I am grateful for the men and women who have labored tirelessly to help us grab hold of our faith in a tangible way. Systematic theology and disciplines are helpful, and I've benefitted from them greatly. But sometimes the system we've created constrains and drains the biblical story of its inherent beauty. And sometimes the rhythms and practices that also form us into the image of Christ get left off the list—including forgiveness.

So in this chapter, I'm being a true Westerner and advocating for forgiveness to be added to the list of spiritual disciplines. And I'm doing this for two reasons: the Lord's Prayer and the role spiritual disciplines are meant to play in our journey of becoming more like

Christ. Let's look at the Lord's Prayer first to see if my argument to include forgiveness as a spiritual discipline is justified.

THE LORD'S PRAYER

In Matthew 6:9-13, Jesus taught His disciples to pray, saying,

> Pray then like this:
>
> "Our Father in heaven,
> hallowed be your name.
> Your kingdom come,
> your will be done,
>   on earth as it is in heaven.
> Give us this day our daily bread,
> and forgive us our debts,
>   as we also have forgiven our debtors.
> And lead us not into temptation,
>   but deliver us from evil."

I want to draw your attention to the phrase "Give us this day our daily bread" (verse 11). Jesus's use of "this day" and "daily" leaves us with the impression that His prayer was meant for daily use. The expectation to pray these words daily would've been assumed by Jesus's disciples even if the "this day" or "daily" were absent. As Jews, their custom was to recite the Shema and other select prayers morning, noon, and night (Deuteronomy 6:4-9). In Luke's Gospel, Jesus precedes His instruction on prayer by saying, "When you pray, say," implying that whenever they went to pray, they were to echo these words to God (Luke 11:2-4). However, these prayers and others like it weren't meant to make for dry or rote times of prayer. Instead, they were meant to be templates to help guide their hearts during prayer.[1]

As those living in a broken world with fallen people, they were taught to make these essential requests to God daily. Each day, in prayer, they needed to remind their souls to worship a holy God who was also their Father. Each day it was necessary for them to call themselves away from the pursuits of building their own kingdom and pray for God's Kingdom to come. Knowing that self-reliance would only get them so far in life, Jesus taught them to ask their heavenly Father to provide for both their physical and spiritual needs. Knowing that on any given day they were liable to sin against Him, He reassured them that it was okay for them to ask the Father daily for the forgiveness of sin. Understanding the persuasiveness of temptation, Jesus encouraged them to pray to not even be led into it.

As I've studied this prayer and started to pray these words almost daily, I've found myself asking: Why did Jesus add "as we also have forgiven our debtors"? Why not just skip to "lead us not into temptation"? Why were these words also daily essentials for His disciples to offer up in prayer as they navigate this world? Was this just a stern reminder of Jesus's expectation for the forgiven to forgive, or was there something more? I believe Jesus added His forgiveness expectation to the disciples' prayer for two reasons: first, to exhort us once again to draw the inspiration and strength we need to forgive others from the forgiveness we've received; and second, to prepare us for another day of living in a broken world with fallen people.

On any given day, not only are we are liable to sin against God, but also someone is liable to sin against us. On any given day, we can find ourselves needing to do the work of forgiveness. Whether it be for a minor offense or a life-altering one, we can find ourselves presented with the opportunity to make the merciful decision to release an offender of a debt and not retaliate against them in anger. By adding "as we also have forgiven our debtors" to our appeals for forgiveness, Jesus is reminding us of this reality. And yes, He is also reminding us of His expectation for the forgiven to forgive. However, this isn't a stern reminder; it flows from His deep and abiding love for you.

Jesus knows what unforgiveness can do to your heart. He knows how unresolved anger can harden your heart, disabling your ability to be loved. People are doing all they can to prove their love for you, but they can't get through. Bitterness has eroded your heart, teaching you to distrust others. Jesus knows how holding on to the pain of offense can lead to chronic anxiety, loneliness, depression, and a host of other health issues. The fear of getting hurt again and never learning how to live beyond offense keeps you from building meaningful relationships with others. He's seen how the refusal to forgive holds someone hostage, stifling their ability to love their neighbor as themselves and love Him.

FORGIVENESS TRANSFORMS US INTO THE IMAGE OF CHRIST

Beloved, if we choose unforgiveness as a way of life, we will inevitably damage our hearts in ways that make it difficult for us to love and be loved by God and others. Forgiveness is a survival skill you must learn so you don't get trapped in bitterness and unresolved anger. It's a habit—a way of life—you must adopt. On any given day, we can be confronted with the opportunity to take up its work. And just like Scripture reading, prayer, fasting, corporate worship, and gospel sharing, we need to make forgiveness our spiritual practice. We need to repent of treating forgiveness as an optional command and start regarding it as spiritual discipline meant to transform us increasingly more into the image of Christ.

Here's my working definition of *spiritual disciplines*: relational rhythms with God *and others* that transform us into the image of Christ. They include spending time with God through Scripture reading, prayer, sitting with Him in silence and solitude, corporate worship, confessing our sins one to another, loving our marginalized neighbor, and faithfully engaging in the work of forgiveness. All of these practices aid us in our ongoing journey of being transformed into the image of Christ. When we forgive, we are taking on the humble mind of Christ as Paul exhorts us to (Philippians 2:5-9). When we forgive, we are taking on the merciful and compassionate heart of God (Psalm 103:8-10). We are forgiving *as* Christ has forgiven us. And I wholeheartedly believe that every time we make the merciful decision to forgive, we become increasingly shaped more into the merciful, loving, and humble character of Christ. Forgiveness transforms us into the image of Christ.

A PROCESS OF FORGIVENESS

If forgiveness is a spiritual discipline, as followers of Jesus Christ, we need to put practical language in place for how to engage in its work. If ever we are confronted with the opportunity to forgive, we need a template to help us move from anger to forgiveness. So, true to my Western form, without making forgiveness a stuffy step-by-step process, I would like to provide a method for how to faithfully engage in the work of forgiveness. The goal here isn't to create a checklist for you, but to make forgiveness practical enough for you to faithfully obey Jesus's command to forgive. Much of this language and process you have engaged with throughout the book. In this chapter, I am only attempting to put it all together.

Honestly Acknowledge

When someone treats you unjustly (or you think they did), you need to selah—to pause and think about what just happened. This may be difficult for those who tend to stuff their feelings or shrug things off by saying, "It is what it is." But this is not how Christ desires for you to respond to offense. He wants you to honestly acknowledge it to ensure bitterness does not seep in, eroding your heart and inhibiting your ability to love God and others. Without ruminating in a way that would only stir up your anger more than settle it, take time to replay what happened. Maybe even write it down. Make a record of what hurt and why. Was it what they said, or that they didn't say anything at all? Was it how they said it that upset you? Identify what you found particularly offensive and how it made you feel. At this part of the process, hold off on making a judgment about how you feel. That will come next. For now, feel what you feel and say what you need to say to God. Let Him be your safe place to vent. If He needs to redirect you, He will.

Search Your Heart

As we saw in chapter 10, sometimes your idols are the source of conflict in your relationships. Because we are just as fallen as the person with whom we've taken offense, we need to be open to the possibility that we may be the source of the problem. We need to heed Jesus's command to pause and consider if there any planks in our eyes and remove those before attempting to remove any specks out of others' eyes (Matthew 7:3-5). We need to invite God to search our hearts and reveal any idolatry in our hearts to determine if the offense is warranted. Sometimes we will discover our offense is warranted, *and* we have an idol throwing gasoline on it, intensifying our response and causing us to overreact. We can be right and wrong at the same time.

Decisively Commit to Forgive

Now that you've made space for God to search your heart and address any planks that might be in your own eye, you are ready to address the speck in your offender's. Of the offenses you noted as you honestly acknowledged what happened and how it made you feel, identify which ones fit under God's law and which fit under your own. Determine which offenses you need to forgive, which ones you need to let go of, and maybe even the ones where you need to extend more grace. Here's a chart to help you discern what kinds of offenses fit in each one of these categories.

Offenses to Forgive	Offenses to Let Go	Offenses Worthy of Extra Grace
Offenses that break God's commands	Pet peeves	When things don't go as planned due to outside factors
Offenses that cross stated and shared values in intimate relationships	Personality differences (These should be discussed so you can grow in understanding, not so you can call a person to repent from being who God made them to be.)	Offenses made during seasons of grief (Though grief doesn't excuse sin, if the person is seasonally struggling and acting out of character, lead with care and concern, not offense.)
Intentional or unintentional offense made due to cultural differences	Miscommunication (If after a thoughtful conversation you learn that your offense is the result of miscommunication, make the decision to let the offense go and work together to create a plan for how to avoid it moving forward.)	Emotional and spiritual maturity (In some cases, particularly in discipleship or relationships where you're the adult or wise auntie, be mindful of the other person's maturity. Part of their behavior speaks to where they are spiritually, not their heart.)
Unintentional and non-sinful offenses that change your life (i.e., accidents that alter your physical well-being, misuse of finances)	Trivial convictions	Offenses made by those who suffer with emotional and mental disorders (Though their sin still hurts and needs to be refined by the grace of the gospel, you must keep in mind how their disorder impacts their ability to love God and others.)

Of the offenses you need to forgive, define what it means for you to forgive by creating a forgiveness resolution. In chapter 5, Reverend Anthony Thompson's forgiveness meant sharing the gospel with Dylann Roof whenever he had an opportunity. Consider what it would mean for you to release your offender of their debt and not retaliate against them. Your resolution could be any of the following:

- I will speak to them when I see them at church.

- I will respond to their text messages and answer their phone calls. I won't necessarily initiate, but I will be responsive.

- I will pray for them.

- I will not speak about their offense with others in our community or publicly.

Humbly Confront

Though I don't want you to move through this process rigidly, I do believe it is helpful to honestly acknowledge and search your heart before you humbly confront. This way you can communicate clearly how the person has wronged you, and you can make sure you don't shortsightedly accuse them, especially when it's possible that you're the guilty party. Honestly acknowledging and searching your heart first can save you from making an emotionally charged response. I also encourage you to decisively commit to forgiving before you humbly confront your offender. This will guard your heart from basing your decision to forgive on their response. Remember that forgiveness is a solo work you do before God. You don't need the other person's apology, shame, or grief to forgive.

Navigating conflict and confronting others comes with a steep learning curve. I could honestly write another book on it, but here are five principles to help get you started:

1. Lead with curiosity.

As my pastor, Ryan Brooks, puts it: "We want to jump to clarity before you jump to conclusions."[2] We do this by asking questions like: "When you said _____, what did you mean?" or "You seemed upset by how I responded to _____. What were you hoping my response would be?" As you ask these questions, pay attention to your tone. Use a curious tone, not a patronizing or accusatory one.

2. Share one offense at a time.

If you've been holding stuff in, you will be tempted to let it all out when you get up the courage to humbly confront. However, this can be unproductive and can cause the person to feel attacked. Bring one offense to their attention at a time so you can articulate it well. Then the two of you can figure out what changes or adjustments need to be made to prevent further offense and move forward in your relationship.

3. Start first.

If, after searching your heart, the Spirit makes you aware of your sin, be the first to apologize. However, don't go into the conversation expecting an apology in return. We don't apologize to manipulate others into apologizing or even recognizing their own sin. If they do, great. But remember, you are primarily apologizing and owning your fault to honor God and Jesus's command to go to those who have something against you (Matthew 5:23-24).

4. Show your feelings without spewing them.

This one is a tricky balance and, depending on your personality, it can be a bit of a learning curve to know how to appropriately put your feelings on display. But the principle here is courageously show your feelings while also being careful to not display those feelings in a way that can be manipulative or counterproductive to moving the conversation forward.

5. Make God's goals your goals.

Remind yourself of God's longing for shalom before, during, and after the conversation. Allow His mission to unite all things in Jesus Christ to inspire your resolve to abandon being shalom-avoidant or shalom-demanding and take up your role as a shalom-maker in the world. Be, as Paul puts it in Ephesians 4:3-4, "eager to maintain the unity of the Spirit in the bond of peace" that Christ created through His blood shed on the cross (Ephesians 2:15-16).

Consider Reconciliation

We talked about this movement at length in the previous chapter, so I won't say much more here than this: Trust Jesus and obey His instruction for how to discern if reconciliation is possible. Commit to humbly confronting those who offend you rather than ignoring offenses and sweeping them under the rug. Commit to bringing trusted others in to mediate the conflict when the two of you can't come to an agreement on your own. In the event the relationship needs to end, commit to leaning in to the counsel and support of a trusted Christ-following community when your offender refuses to listen.

Practice Trust

If your offender listens by confessing their sins against you and making noticeable steps of forgiveness, your shared work will be rebuilding trust in the relationship. We will discuss more of when and how to do this in the last section of this book. But for now, let's selah before we move on to the next part, "When It Hurts So Bad," to talk about anger and abuse. If hearing the story of sexual abuse would be disarming for you, please consider skipping the first paragraph of the section's opener.

1 **Honestly Acknowledge**
Tell the truth about what happened, name the offense, and put words to the pain it has caused.

2 **Search Your Heart**
Invite God to inspect your heart to discern any sin or short-sightedness on your part.

3 **Decisively Commit to Forgive**
Make the merciful decision to forgive and make your forgiveness resolutions.

4 **Humbly Confront**
Go to your offender humbly pointing out their offense.

5 **Consider Reconciliation**
Follow Jesus's instructions in Matthew 18:15-20 to discern if reconciliation is possible.

6 **Practice Trust**
Explore what's relationally possible.

SELAH: For this selah, let's pray through the prayer Jesus taught His disciples in Matthew 6:9-13:

[9] Pray then like this:

"Our Father in heaven,
   hallowed be your name.
[10] Your kingdom come,
   your will be done,
      on earth as it is in heaven.
[11] Give us this day our daily bread,
[12] and forgive us our debts,
      as we also have forgiven our debtors.

[13] And lead us not into temptation,
       but deliver us from evil."

READ: Read Matthew 6:9-13 slowly and pause over any words or phrases that stand out to you.

REFLECT: Read Matthew 6:9-13 slowly again. Consider how this prayer helps orient our hearts as we navigate the reality of living in a broken world with fallen people who await their future home.

RESPOND: Invite God's Spirit to search your heart as you consider the following questions.

- Which of the movements in the process of forgiveness would be most challenging for you and why?

- Is there anyone in your life who excels in this challenge? If so, how can you intentionally invite them to help you grow in this area?

REST: Slowly pray this prayer to God. Use it as a template, adding your own lines and inserting the cares and needs at the top of your heart. Confess your sins and ask for more grace to forgive.

PART 4

WHEN IT HURTS SO BAD

I left her room speechless. For the first time in ministry, I didn't know what to say or how to say it. I was clueless of how to sit with her pain and assure her God was good. She had been raped. Sexually assaulted by someone she trusted. Taken advantage of by someone she hoped to one day hold hands with and say I do. For months, she had been keeping her trauma concealed, and now, with tearful eyes, she was trusting me with it. She could keep it to herself no longer. She needed comfort. She needed answers.

After she shared, silence filled the air as we held each other's tearful gaze. To myself, I prayed and asked God to give me words. I wanted so badly to say something helpful, but as I skimmed through my mental Rolodex of what I'd heard others say to someone who's experienced abuse, nothing felt right.

Joseph's "As for you, you meant evil against me, but God meant it for good" (Genesis 50:20) felt shortsighted. Sure, this verse might've offered a shortcut to some semblance of comfort and saved me from engaging her questioning and pain, but in the long run, it was sure to bring up more questions—such as: "How could a good God mean *this* for my good?" or "Does God care more about His redemptive bottom line than my personal well-being?"

Paul's "We know that for those who love God all things work together for good" (Romans 8:28) didn't seem appropriate either. Albeit true, this didn't feel like the ideal time to state this truth. Right now she was in excruciating emotional pain. I'm also sure that if she had been given the choice, she would've opted out of any good that could come from this kind of evil.

The preacher's redemptive "He'll give you double for your trouble" based on the ending of the book of Job seemed ill-placed. Her suffering and Job's were qualitatively different. I've also never been confident that Job would've adopted this verbiage to make sense of his own story. He possibly would've even found these words offensive. How could the grief of losing 7 children be so easily relieved with the gift of having 14 more?

But the book of Job did offer me some wisdom—not by giving me words to say, but by reminding me to sit with my friend in silence, bearing witness to her pain and not leaving her to lament alone. Like many who experience abuse, she shifted blame from her abuser to herself, listing off all the things she could've or should've done differently. In that moment, what she needed the most was not a pithy catchall statement to temporarily pacify her pain. She needed someone to bear witness to her pain by being "present and attentive to the truth" of her experience.[1] She needed someone to tell her it wasn't her fault. She needed someone to affirm her pain and assure her that she was precious, loved, and worth so much more than the horror she experienced. She needed someone to acknowledge the courage it took for her to say what happened out loud. She needed the gentle touch of a friend. She would need all of these things to honestly acknowledge she had been violated, to then confront her abuser by filing a sexual assault report with the police.

This would be the first of several other occasions I would be invited to bear witness to the pain of sexual abuse. Over the past 20 years of ministry, I have heard the horrors of women and men who have suffered not only sexual abuse, but also physical, emotional, and spiritual abuse. I count it a painful privilege to be invited to walk with people in the valley of suffering and healing from abuse. But every time I find myself in this particular valley, it unsettles my faith. I'm left crying out to God, asking:

> *Lord, how do people move forward in life after enduring this kind of pain?*

> *God, why did You allow this to happen?*

> *These are good people who love You! Obey You! How could You let someone not only do this to them, but get away with it?*

In this section, I want to share truths that have helped settle my faith when it's gotten unsettled. I want to offer a way forward for those who've experienced abuse and are struggling to forgive. However, I know for some this may *feel* uncomfortable and insensitive. What happened to you was evil. And to ask or expect you to forgive seems extremely unfair and unreasonable. I hear you, and in many ways I agree. But, friend, remember, we do not forgive others because they deserve it. They don't. We forgive because Jesus commands it. But He doesn't command it as One who doesn't care about the abuse you've endured. He commands it as One who is ever acquainted with the pain of abuse and as One who, as we will see in this section, will execute justice on your behalf.

In this section, I also want to offer a way forward for those whose greatest barrier to forgive is their anger. The story of the hardest person

I have ever had to forgive is not in the pages of this book. Part of what it means for me to forgive them is not to share their offense publicly. They're forgiven, we've reconciled, and we are living beyond offense as best we can. But it was my anger that made it difficult to make the onetime merciful decision to forgive and the continuous decision to faithfully cast their forgiven offenses back into the depths of the sea.

Our primary text for this section will be Psalm 37. It was this psalm that provided my heart with a road map for how to move through my anger and to forgive my offender. It's also in this psalm that I find no better words to offer to those who've suffered abuse. If you've suffered abuse or are consumed with anger, I pray this psalm will help you as much as it's helped me.

CHAPTER 12

LIVING BEYOND ANGER

Fret not yourself because of evildoers.

PSALM 37:1

*S*ome offenses don't just hurt your feelings; they change your life. These aren't the ones that temporarily unsettle your nerves or set you back emotionally for a few months. They interrupt your plotline, altering the trajectory of your story.

- Though you both vowed your only cause of separation would be death, your spouse's infidelity and lack of repentance has ended your marriage and left you and your children with scars your love cannot fully heal.

- Their spousal abandonment has resulted in decades of loneliness. You were never fortunate to find that spark with someone new, and now that you're nearing the end of your life, you wonder who will be with you when you take your last breath.

- You embarked on what was supposed to be the business venture of a lifetime with a friend, and it resulted in financial betrayal. You've lost your friend, your business, and the hope of ever being in a financial position to try again.

- You were hopeful that the person who offered to disciple you would help build your faith, but instead they crushed it with their pride, unreasonable expectations, and spiritual abuse. You've lost all faith in the church and are even disillusioned with Christ.

- Before your story even got started, someone dismantled your innocence. Not only is your body riddled with trauma, but you've also adopted unhealthy and unwanted coping mechanisms that seem impossible to break. The emotional, physical, or sexual abuse didn't just wound you; it changed you.

If you have experienced a life-altering offense, and even if you agree with the concepts of forgiveness discussed in this book, it may still seem impossible to forgive. To make the merciful decision to release your offender from the just punishment they deserve and not retaliate against them in anger feels like an act of treason against yourself or someone you deeply love. How could you possibly let it go or let them go free? And how could a good God expect you to?

It sounds unfair. But I pray that as we walk through the wisdom in Psalm 37:1-9, you will find good cause for letting go of your anger and forgive. But first, let's have a quick talk about anger.

WHAT IS ANGER?

Anger is primarily concerned with two things—what we love and what we hate. It's our justice emotion, standing ready to defend and vindicate our loves. When someone or something we love is being treated in a way that we hate, our anger lights its match. Counselors J. Aladair Groves and Winston T. Smith explain that anger happens when "your heart is observing [or experiencing] the scene before you and crying out that something you love is being treated unjustly."[1]

Though anger can often be classified as a negative and even sinful emotion, it is a good and healthy one. It's also an appropriate and needed one for those living in a broken world with fallen people. On any given day, anger may call upon us to *humbly confront* those who act unjustly toward us or our neighbor. On any given day, anger may be needed to move our hearts, hands, and feet to help defend and protect the vulnerable. However, anger is only good and healthy when it aligns with what God loves and hates.

When what we love and what we hate are rooted in the moral character of God, our anger testifies to the truth that we are created in the image of a righteous and holy God. But if not, it reveals, as we discussed in chapter 10, that our loves are disordered and inordinate. But when our hearts are indeed observing or experiencing injustice, our anger should kindle and burn. We should be angry at the injustice committed against us or others. Anger is an appropriate response when someone lies, steals, cheats, or takes advantage of us. Anger is warranted when a parent or spouse abandons, a friend betrays, or ministry leader abuses. And just as God shares our longing for shalom when we suffer offense, He shares our anger.

God loves you. His anger is kindled and burns every time someone He lovingly created in His image is treated unjustly. He shares your anger for offenses committed against you. And like any self-respecting parent, He is likely angrier than you are.

If He hates sin, you can hate it. If He's angry, you can be angry as well. It's justifiable and expected. We are created in His image, and we are called to live out His moral character in His world. Your anger toward evil—sin run amok—is good. However, anger run amok is not.

If we allow our anger to burn too long, it can erode our hearts, causing us to commit the sins of bitterness, resentment, malice, slander, and unforgiveness. If we don't contain it, it can cause us to harm innocent others. This is why Paul encourages us to "be angry and do not sin" and to "not let the sun go down on your anger" (Ephesians 4:26).

Anger doesn't hold well. Like anxiety, it is a viscerally intense emotion that radiates its impulse up and down your body. It's like a toddler that can't keep still and must be put to bed. It will not do it on its own. It will keep getting out of bed, restlessly looking for a place to extinguish itself. Even when its desired target is not within reach, it will settle for another. It can also be dangerous if untamed, leading to violence and harm. It's action-oriented, demanding, and seeks resolve quickly. It doesn't naturally stop to selah.

MOVING FROM ANGER TO FORGIVENESS

Paul's instruction to be angry and don't sin falls into the easier-said-than-done category of life. But in Psalm 37, King David provides us with a road map for how to move through our anger to forgiveness. He invites us to selah—to pause and think—before we follow our anger's suggestion to retaliate and seek justice with our own hands or on our own terms. Though he understands our desire to do so, he encourages us to choose a different path by providing us with six places to redirect our anger when it reaches its full, can't-be-quieted capacity and is getting in position to retaliate against an offender. In this chapter we will look at the first three places he encourages us to redirect our anger. In the next chapter, we will explore the remaining three as they offer reassuring news for the abused. And along the way, following the flow of the passage, we will sit with David's one compelling reason for why we can redirect our anger.

Fret Not Yourself

> *Fret not yourself because of evildoers;*
> *be not envious of wrongdoers!*
> **PSALM 37:1**

What's been translated in our Bibles as *fret* means to "be angry, aroused, burn with anger, have a temper, i.e., have a strong feeling of displeasure, with a focus of an action to follow."[2] This definition is vastly different from the picture that comes to mind when we read the word *fret*. When I think of someone fretting, I envision them cowering in a corner shaking. Consumed with fear, they are unable and unwilling to move from their current position of real or perceived safety. Or maybe they're frantically pacing, ruminating on what happened. They walk in circles around their fear, trying to discern what they could've done differently to protect themselves. However, the picture David is seeking to paint here isn't of a person cowering in a corner with uncontrollable shakes. Instead, the picture is of someone standing on the precipice of being fully controlled by their anger. Their chest is heaving, their fists are balled up tight, and their feet are ready to run headfirst in the direction of their offender. All they see is red. And if they are frantically pacing, it isn't because they are ruminating on what happened. It's because they are plotting what they will do next. They walk in circles trying to discern how they will get their offender back. Will their next move be a sly comment, or will they slash their offender's tires? Can they devise a plan to drag their name through the mud to shame them the same way they were shamed? Would having an affair settle the score and help their spouse understand the pain of betrayal?

As Peter C. Craigie explains, there is a "natural temptation" to want to get somebody back for the pain they've caused.[3] They have disrupted your sense of safety, security, and shalom, and now you want to disrupt theirs. However, King David exhorts us to resign from this temptation for this one compelling reason: Justice will prevail.

> For they will soon fade like the grass and wither like the green herb (Psalm 37:2).

If this psalm is a song, this refrain is its chorus. Repeatedly, David weaves the truth that justice will prevail in between his encouragement to "fret not," "trust in the LORD, and do good," "refrain from anger" and give up your rage (verses 1, 3, 8). He constantly reminds the one who is longing for justice of the wicked's fate:

> Psalm 37:9: "For the evildoers shall be cut off."
>
> Psalm 37:10: "In just a little while, the wicked will be no more; though you look carefully at his place, he will not be there."
>
> Psalm 37:20: "The wicked will perish...like smoke they vanish."
>
> Psalm 37:38: "Transgressors shall be altogether destroyed; the future of the wicked shall be cut off."

This refrain is repeated throughout this psalm because there is no other justifiable reason to cease one's fretting except knowing that justice will inevitably prevail. The psalmist knows that the only way for you to find a way out of your restless agitation and move toward shalom is to have certainty that the person or people who abused you will "fade like grass." Though justice may not come swiftly or visibly, you can know it will come surely. Though the police didn't believe you, your church didn't take the appropriate actions, and the court didn't rule in your favor, you can have confidence your offender's presumed victory will "wither like the green herb." Their injustice will not prevail; justice will. You don't need to fret, and you don't have to retaliate, which is why in the next verses, David redirects us from spending our energy fretting toward trusting God and doing good.

Trust and Do Good

> *Trust in the LORD, and do good; dwell in*
> *the land and befriend faithfulness.*
>
> **PSALM 37:3**

David has yet to reveal the source from which this certain justice will come from, but later he will explain that it's not the gravitational pull of karma or the universe putting evildoers in their place. It is the very activity of God. He is the source of our certain justice. And because we know His justice is certain we can stop fretting, trust Him to put evildoers in their place, and do good. We can, as my friend and writing coach Chris Pappalardo wrote in the margin of this section's draft, "Lay aside our (wrong) role as judge, entrust justice to the God, the true judge, and focus on our responsibility—living faithfully before him."[4]

Though what it means to "do good" in the wake of an offense isn't clarified here, it is clear in Jesus's teaching. To do good is to do the hard work of turning the other cheek. To do good is to resist the innate temptation to retaliate. To do good is to do what feels unnatural and pray for the repentance and shalom of the person who hurt you. It's to bombard heaven with your cries for justice and requests for your offender to confess their sins and repent. To do good is to forgive as you have been forgiven.

He calls you to not allow your anger to determine your next steps, and instead, be controlled by the truth that God's justice will prevail, not the lie that the person who harmed you will get away with it.

Delight Yourself in the Lord

Delight yourself in the LORD, and he will give you the desires of your heart.

PSALM 37:4

Like most, I have racked my brain trying to discern the meaning of this verse. Is it "if I delight myself in the Lord, He will give me what I desire"? or is it "if I delight myself in the Lord, He will place what He desires in my heart"? However, given the context, this concern is irrelevant. We know what the person the psalmist is speaking to wants. Their heart isn't fretting over a new car, a new job, or a relationship. Their heart is fretting over a desire for justice. Psalm 37 has also been recognized among the list of imprecatory psalms where the biblical author's primary concern is justice.

Please don't miss this context. In fact, this is so critical (and so easy to miss) that I'm going to paraphrase these verses for you. Here's how you should read this: "Delight yourself in the Lord, and he will satisfy your desire for justice."

Beloved, I know you're angry. You have a right to be. What someone did was wrong, sinful, and unjust. God is angry alongside you. Embrace this invitation to trade your restless fretting for delighting in the character and presence of God. Let the truths that He is holy, sovereign, and just, fortify your confidence in His ability to execute justice on your behalf. Let the reality of His never-ending love for you and commitment to justice extinguish and put your anger to rest.

SELAH: For this selah, let's put to practice the wisdom we just discussed in Psalm 37:1-4:

> [1] Fret not yourself because of evildoers;
>   be not envious of wrongdoers!
> [2] For they will soon fade like the grass
>   and wither like the green herb.
> [3] Trust in the LORD, and do good;
>   dwell in the land and befriend faithfulness.
> [4] Delight yourself in the LORD,
>   and he will give you the desires of your heart.

READ: Read Psalm 37:1-4 slowly and pause over any words or phrases that stand out to you.

REFLECT: Read Psalm 37:1-4 slowly again. Consider what causes you to fret the most about the injustice you've experienced. Make a list of all the things that make you angry, adding the reason why when possible.

RESPOND: Read Psalm 37:1-4 slowly again, pausing over verses 3 and 4. Consider what it looks like for you to respond to the instruction in these verses.

- Knowing that justice will prevail, what does it look like for you to obey the command to "do good" without putting yourself in danger or overly forcing yourself to take a step you're not ready to take? It will feel unnatural, but consider a faithful step of obedience you can take not a forceful one. Remember, we can only live up to that which we've obtained (Philippians 3:15-16).

- In what ways can you delight in the presence and character of God to fortify your confidence that He will execute justice on your behalf?

REST: Ask God to give you the grace to cease fretting and rest. Take a few long deep breaths, picturing yourself releasing your fretting with each exhale and taking in the shalom of God's presence with each inhale.

CHAPTER 13

LIVING BEYOND ABUSE

He will bring forth your righteousness as the light,
and your justice as the noonday.

PSALM 37:6

I n this chapter, we are going to continue our journey through the wisdom found in Psalm 37:1-9, looking at it through the lens of abuse. However, even if you haven't experienced abuse, this chapter also has good news for you. It has good news for everyone who has ever experienced the suffering of offense.

As I briefly mentioned in the previous chapter, Psalm 37 is an imprecatory psalm. In our Bibles you will find more than 20 of them.[1] As sojourners, living in a broken world with fallen people, the psalmists often call out to God for rescue, comfort, and relief. Throughout their life they have lived under these three presuppositions: (1) God is good; (2) God rewards the righteous; (3) God punishes the wicked. However, as they look out into the world they are tempted to believe a different story. It's the wicked, not the righteous, who appear to be like a lush tree that bears fruit season after season (Psalm 1:1-3). It's evildoers who always seem to prosper in their way, and the psalmists are mad. I'm talking *big mad*. Their longing for justice has given rise to their anger. Someone they love has been treated in a way they hate. Their hearts have witnessed someone they love being treated unjustly. Their anger is appropriate.

However, if you're like me, when you read one of these angry psalms, their cries to God don't sound appropriate. In fact, it feels very inappropriate. Is it seriously okay to pray, "Punish them, God; let them fall by their own schemes"? (Psalm 5:10) Could I get in trouble for asking God to "knock the teeth out" of someone's mouth? (Psalm 58:6). This rhetoric sounds like the opposite of shalom-making.

BEYOND THE OFFENSE

Despite how unsettling these psalms sound, they provide us with three helpful starting points for how to live beyond the offense of abuse:

1. Say what you need to say.

The writers of these imprecatory psalms don't hold back. They speak honestly about the pain and anger they feel. This pattern is consistent throughout these psalms and teaches us that we can and need to honestly acknowledge the pain, frustration, and anger we feel. We need to, as Pastor Christian White says, "Feel what we feel and tell the truth about it."[2]

2. Say what you need to say to God.

Almost nowhere in the Bible do we find people hiding what they feel from God. Instead, they pour out their heart to Him fully. Even when they are in the wrong and suffering as a result of their own sin, they unashamedly confess their pain, frustration, and anger to God. They make God a refuge for any and everything they feel.

Beloved, you can and need to say what you need to say and to say it to God. These two steps are integral to your healing. You can't heal from what you are unwilling to acknowledge. God's love, though ever flowing in your direction, can't touch what you keep covered. In order to get out of the prison someone's abuse may have put you in, you have to let God in to heal you and show you the way out.

3. Appeal to God for justice.

In each of these psalms, the writers call out to God for justice. However, they never ask God for the strength or opportunity to smite their enemies. Instead, they call on God, who always judges justly, to settle their case. They don't try to seek recompense or execute justice by their own power and will. They leave that work to God.

True to the imprecatory genre's form, David invites us to do all three of these things in his next redirect. But before we make our way there, I feel the need to address the uncomfortable irony that these words come from a sexual abuser.

WHY SHOULD WE LISTEN TO DAVID?

David is by far one of the most complex characters in the Bible. In his life, he has been both the offended and the offender, the perpetrator and the victim, the abused and the abuser. He is an imperfect mixed bag of courage and cowardice, faithfulness and faithlessness, doing the right thing and terribly doing the wrong thing.

Toward the end of this psalm, David alludes to his old age, saying: "I have been young, and now am old, yet I have not seen the righteous forsaken or his children begging for bread" (Psalm 37:25). Given his history, it's hard to imagine that David is only saying this as someone who has experienced injustice. After being confronted by Nathan for his sexual abuse against Bathsheba and the murder of her husband, Uriah, David's life was a downward spiral. Though he quickly repented and the Lord forgave him, justice still prevailed. And it was painful for him and the many innocent others in his family. Bathsheba lost her first born. His son Amnon followed in his sinful footsteps and raped David's daughter, Tamar. As an act of retaliation against Amnon and David, Absalom, David's other son, killed Amnon and took over David's kingdom. Then Absalom sexually abused each of David's concubines in broad daylight. And all this happened just as Nathan prophesied it would, serving as God's judgment against David for his sin (1 Samuel 12:11-12). So I don't imagine David as an old man, sitting in his rocker contemplating about life, and writing this psalm absent of his own acts of injustice. He has seen God's justice prevail in his favor when King Saul sought to kill him and when God's justice was against him for his sin. And it is from this lived experience that he gives us this psalm, exhorting us to trade our justified but restless fretting for trusting God to satisfy our desire for justice. And to this exhortation he provides three more places for us to redirect our anger.

Entrust Your Case to the Lord

> *Commit your way to the LORD;*
> *trust in him, and he will act.*

PSALM 37:5

In Hebrew, this call to commit your way to the Lord means "to roll" your restless agitation for justice off your shoulders into the capable hands of God. It is to, as the saints at my home church would sing, "lay your burdens down." To cease your fretting and find relief in the truth that God will act.

However, for those who have experienced injustice or abuse, there is a very valid and commonsense question hanging over this invitation to trust God. *Why can we trust God to act now, when He did not act then?*

While there are some who don't need an answer to this question, I know there are many who do. Your first questions to God after *it* happened were: "Why?," "God, where were You?," and "How could You, in Your sovereignty and goodness, allow this to happen?" The idea of trusting God with your life or entrusting Him with your case is out of reach. Before you can "roll over" your cares into the hands of God, you need to be reassured that He cares. Only then will you be able to trade your restless agitation for rest in God.

Here are a just a few of the truths that have helped me wrestle well with these questions and put trusting God within reach amid suffering:

1. We were made for shalom.

We discussed this truth early on in chapter 1 to help us make sense of why being sinned against hurts so bad, but this truth also helps us to hold on to an accurate view of God amid suffering. In Genesis 1–2, we find God's heart. He created us to safely live and thrive in a lush garden filled with His glory and shalom. Even though the world is broken, this was not His original design or intention for us. We will need to tighten our grip on this truth when our lived experience deviates from the shalom we were made for. If we don't, suffering will lure us into the belief that God is neither trustworthy nor good. But He is the God of shalom, not the author of brokenness, suffering, or abuse. We can trust that what's become broken, He will make whole.

2. The problem of evil doesn't reveal a problem with God; it reveals a problem with humanity.

Sin, in all its variations, exists because of human rebellion, not because God's power is insufficient, or His love is absent. As New Testament scholar Dr. Esau McCaulley explains,

> God created a world [in which] we can choose to love one another, and that's what makes life beautiful. But in a world where you can choose to love one another, you can also choose to do harm. And when you have a world that is broken because of sin, some people will choose to love and some will choose to do harm…Suffering doesn't exist because God wills evil, but [because] part of the human experience allows for the possibility of evil.[3]

When asking the question "God, why did You let this happen?," we have to be careful to not shift the blame that belongs to the one who sinned against us to God. We must remember that we live in a broken world with fallen people. Beloved, this is the problem that gives rise to the evil you've suffered, not a lack of God's love, care, or concern for you.

3. Jesus entered and endured our broken world with fallen people.

Jesus entered our world and became like us. He could've entered the world as One above it, but "for a little while" He became a little lower than the angels (Hebrews 2:9). He took on human fragility so He could fully understand the struggles of living in this world. He endured a life of poverty and social scrutiny so He could identify with the pain of the marginalized and oppressed. He wanted them to know that even if the world doesn't see them, He sees them. He suffered emotional and physical abuse so He could say "I understand" to those who have experienced the same. And in His death, He bore the pain of feeling abandoned by God. He cried out, "My God, my God, why have you forsaken me?," letting us all know that it's okay to do the same (Matthew 27:46). Even though in His divinity, Jesus knew the answer to these questions, in His humanity, He couldn't resist asking. However, there was no response from heaven. No, "This is my Son with whom I am well pleased" or "This is my Son, listen to Him" resounding from heaven. Jesus knows the pain of asking God "why" and being met with silence. Though we might not get the answers to our questions, in Christ, we get, as Dr. Christina Edmondson puts it, "a solidarity of experience."[4] Jesus entered our world and endured its suffering. He did not remain above it. He is Emmanuel—God with us.

4. God hates suffering, injustice, and sexual abuse.

Many are uncomfortable with the stories of sexual abuse in the Bible, but I'm personally grateful they are there. They testify to a God who does not cover His eyes and look away. They reveal to us that our God is neither absent, aloof, nor indifferent to sexual abuse. No! He is the God of Hagar who sees. He is the God of Bathsheba who confronts. He is the God of the Levite's concubine who sets a whole nation straight because of the unjust society they created that gave way to her abuse and death. These stories have been recorded in our Bibles not to imply in any way that God condones sexual abuse, but to teach us He outright condemns it. In each instance, it is deemed as a wicked, sinful, and evil outrage. In every ungodly occurrence, though sometimes confusing and not readily understood, justice was served. Though each of these stories could've been left out of the biblical record, He leaves them in to assure those who have suffered injustice and abuse they can entrust their case to Him. He will act on their behalf.

To reassure us of this, David returns to his chorus of this psalm: "He will bring forth *your* righteousness as the light, and *your* justice as the noonday" (Psalm 37:6, emphasis added). This verse could've easily been written "God will bring forth His righteousness as light, and His justice as the noonday" to give the reader assurance that God will bring about justice for His name's sake, but it's not written that way. Instead, the possessive pronoun used here is "your." It is *your* righteousness and *your* justice that will shine like the noonday sun. The righteousness and justice that will come is personal; it will be uniquely connected to your case. It's not merely His name He seeks to vindicate, it's also yours. He sees. He cares. His heart has observed the scenes of abuse you've experienced and because He loves you with a jealous and righteous love, He is grieved, angry, and personally invested in your case. You can roll it over to Him, resting fully assured that He will act on *your* behalf. Justice will prevail.

Even though justice didn't prevail in the courts of this world, your justice will prevail in the courts of heaven. Your God doesn't need the justice system to execute justice on your behalf. He is the sovereign

King, who rules over the heavens and the earth. He is the righteous Judge, who holds all offenders accountable for their sins. Even though it appears that your offender is prospering in their way, you can rest assured justice is coming. It is merely delayed. God will "bring forth your righteousness as the light, and your justice as the noonday." But, keep in mind, the operative word here is the future tense "will." There will be some waiting. Though it may seem like the one who has hurt you is getting on with their life, remember justice has merely been delayed, not denied.

Rest and Wait on the Lord

> Be still before the LORD and wait patiently for him;
> fret not yourself over the one who prospers in his
> way, over the man who carries out evil devices!
>
> **PSALM 37:7**

Again, telling anger to wait patiently is like asking a toddler to keep still. It's counterintuitive. As counselors Groves and Smith write in *Untangling Emotions*, "Anger wants results fast."[5] To delay your anger's gratification is to put it in a constant state of fretting.

I pray our journey through this psalm has, at the very least, helped you understand and accept *why* you can wait. Justice will prevail. However, I know that understanding *why* you can wait is not the same as knowing *how* to do it. The latter is much harder. But what I appreciate so much about this psalm is that David tells us how to wait. The call to wait isn't because David or God is putting you and your anger in a time out until you can change your attitude. You're not being told to passively sit in a corner. This would only cause you to fret more, ruminating on the injustice committed against you and the pain caused because of it. To redirect you from this, you've been exhorted to trust God and do good, delight in His presence and character, and entrust your case to Him. This waiting isn't passive. It's active. And, if I could, I would like to add that during your waiting you also make yourself available for the healing process.

Like the writers of the imprecatory psalms, we also need *to say what we need to say and say it to God*, and we need to keep saying it to Him until, like a restless child, we can put our anger to bed. This is *not* easy. Remember, anger is a viscerally intense emotion that radiates its impulses up and down your body. So, in addition to saying what you need to say and saying what you need to say to God, you may also need to move.

When I'm angry, I walk. For miles and miles, I say what I need to say, trying to get some of the angst out of my body. When I can't walk, I step away and take a deep breath. And I've been known to go and hide in a bathroom to do this when I'm at work or in a public place. I also journal. The act of writing helps get emotions out in ways that praying in my mind or out loud cannot. Like the writers of the imprecatory psalms, through paper and pen I say what I need to say to God, pouring out my heart God unfiltered. He sees my thoughts anyway so there is no need to hide them.

Friends, this is what we do in the waiting. We turn over our anger to God as much as needed. We take up practices like moving our bodies, deep breathing, journaling, and others to help slow down our anger so that in the waiting for justice we don't stay in a constant state of fretting or retaliate in anger.

Don't Retaliate in Anger

Refrain from anger, and forsake wrath!
Fret not yourself; it tends only to evil.
PSALM 37:8

The command to "refrain from anger, and forsake wrath" is a loving one. If you leave your anger unresolved, you are likely to give in to it. In your attempts to hold your offender accountable for their acts of self-conscious, self-centered self-preservation, you will commit your own. Your demands for your shalom to be restored will only lead to more brokenness, more evilness, more sin run amok. And, as Chris Pappalardo once again pointed out in my draft's margin, "in so doing, your anger will not grow *less*, but *more*. This is the irony in feeding your anger. It's like a fire: When you feed it, it grows."[6]

This is the tragic tale of Absalom, David's son. Though his anger for the injustice done against his sister, Tamar, was justified, what he did in response was unjust. And with each act of vengeance, his anger grew, compelling him to commit one offense after another. So blinded by his anger, in seeking to humiliate his father, Absalom became like his brother Amnon. Proving the words in James 1:20 to be true— "The anger of [humans] does not produce the righteousness of God."

Again, you and I are not good judges. When anger is seated at the judge's bench of our heart dictating our decision-making or in the driver's seat dictating its pace, we are liable to go too far. Though our anger is warranted, when it's not submitted to God, it will take two eyes for an eye and a whole row of teeth for the loss of one. It will take us further than we want to go, not only getting back at our offender, but also sinning against God and, in some cases, innocent others.

And this is why I consider this command, and all the ones proceeding, to be filled with love. It's a warning. If you don't refrain from your anger, and you allow your wrath to determine your next steps, you will be judged alongside your offender. Just as God will hold them accountable for their sin, He will hold you accountable for yours. Retaliation is not the path you are called to take and remember it's not the one you have to take to ensure your justice and righteousness shines like the noonday sun. God will take care of that. And while He's doing that, take your rest.

Sensing our need to hear the chorus again in order to take our rest, David returns to his justice will prevail refrain. But this time he adds another compelling reason to cease our fretting: "For the evildoers shall be cut off, but those who wait for the Lord shall inherit the land" (Psalm 37:8-9). Not only will God execute justice on your behalf, He will also restore you. God will heal you. He will restore shalom and flourishing to your body, mind, and soul. However, this will be a process. Your shalom has been traumatized, and in the conditions of a fallen and broken world, it will take time to heal. But God can and will progressively heal you as you make yourself available to the healing process. We will talk more about how to make yourself available to the healing process in final section of this book. But for now, I just want to stand as a witness to this truth. I have seen Him do it with my very own eyes as I've walked with those who've suffered abuse. Their lives are full and they live with a kind of freedom that's evident they fought for it.

Beloved, God wants to heal, and He will. He will cause your righteousness and your justice to shine as brightly as the noonday sun. While He's wielding justice on your behalf, trade your fretting for trusting God and doing good. Delight in His presence and character, knowing He will satisfy your desire for justice. Say what you need to say and entrust your case fully into His capable hands. Be still and wait for His timing, being assured that justice is merely delayed not denied. Refrain from trying to wield justice with your own hands.

SELAH: For this selah, let's pause to consider how to apply the wisdom shared with us Psalm 37:5-9:

> [5] Commit your way to the Lord;
>   trust in him, and he will act.
> [6] He will bring forth your righteousness as the light,
>   and your justice as the noonday.
> [7] Be still before the Lord and wait patiently for him;
>   fret not yourself over the one who prospers in his way,

over the man who carries out evil devices!
[8] Refrain from anger, and forsake wrath!
    Fret not yourself; it tends only to evil.
[9] For the evildoers shall be cut off,
    but those who wait for the LORD shall inherit the land.

READ: Read Psalm 37:5-9 slowly and pause over any words or phrases that stand out to you.

REFLECT: Read Psalm 37:5-9 slowly again. Consider why it may be difficult for you to entrust your case to the Lord. Write out the ways you are struggling to trust Him.

RESPOND: Read Psalm 37:5-9 slowly again. Consider what it looks like for you to respond to the instruction in these verses.

- How will you actively "be still before the LORD and wait patiently on him"?

- Have you been tempted in any way to wield justice by your own hands? If so, how and what does it look like to instead trust in the Lord and do good?

REST: Read Psalm 37:7 again. Ask God to give you the grace to cease fretting and be still and rest in Him. Consider how you might need to move your body, say what you need to Him, or make yourself available to the healing to redirect your anger and cease fretting.

PART 5

TRUSTING AGAIN

I signed the contract to write this book with tears. Surrounded by close friends, we thanked God and prayed for the journey of writing ahead. While I was grateful for their presence, I couldn't shake the ache of who wasn't there. I had been abandoned again. But this time by a friend who I never thought of as a seasonal friend. We were sisters and declared it to be fact anytime someone said we looked alike. Even now, as I write, I'm still dizzy with confusion as to why our friendship ended. Its unique and abrupt ending didn't leave much space to get clarity or ask follow-up questions. And unfortunately, we didn't get an opportunity to apply many of the principles that have been laid out in this book. It was just over, and now, I had to do the work of forgiveness.

While forgiveness was work I was willing to do, I wasn't really open to doing the work of trusting again. I was good. I had my hilarious, kind, and trustworthy cohort of good friends and was in no need of looking for new ones. With them not only did I feel safe, but I was safe. They weren't perfect, but when we hurt one another, we made space to hear grievances, confess sin, swap heartfelt apologies, and figure out how one or both of us needed to repent to love each other better. Plus, after experiencing a handful of friendships lost and even more friendship shifts, I wasn't sure if my heart could take the pain of more loss.

In her book *I Love You, But I Don't Trust You*, couple and family therapist Mira Kirshenbaum explains that when someone breaks our trust "it's like going through an earthquake...in a place where you thought there weren't any earthquakes."[1] When my friend ended our friendship, it felt like going through an earthquake in a place I never expected to experience an earthquake. Sure, our friendship had endured challenges and wasn't as easy as it had been in the past, but due to the sisterhood we shared, I trusted that we would always give each other the benefit of the doubt, do the work required to keep our relationship intact, and never leave one another.

Friends, in this broken world, people will break our trust. Their offenses will set off earthquakes in places we never expected. Like an earthquake, when trust is broken, there are aftershocks and ripple effects that go way beyond the relationship of its origin. In the aftermath, we are left with the work of restoring our ability to trust, as we wrestle with the questions:

Can I ever trust them again?
Can I trust anybody?
Can I trust myself?
Can I trust God?

In this section, I want to help you discern the answer to the first question and assure you that the answer to the following three questions is yes. But, first let's define trust.

CHAPTER 14

WHAT IS TRUST?

Unless I see in his hands the mark of the nails, and
place my finger into the mark of the nails, and
place my hand into his side, I will never believe.

THOMAS, JOHN 20:25

In his book *Trust*, clinical psychologist and boundaries expert Dr. Henry Cloud describes trust as the ability to be "careless" with someone. He writes, when we trust someone, we can be "careless in the sense of not having to 'take care' of yourself...we can forget about having to watch our back or watch out for whatever we have entrusted to them. We feel like we don't have a care in the world."[1]

Dr. Cloud's definition of trust as the ability to be "careless" with someone reminds me of the beautiful naked and unashamed reality Adam and Eve enjoyed in the garden. In a world filled with shalom and absent of sin, they enjoyed the gift of being vulnerable with one another without reservation or fear. Neither of them had to watch their backs or be careful or measured in their interactions with one another. For them, trusting one another wasn't a risk. It was a gift. It granted them the benefit of never feeling emotionally alone. All their needs and interests were shared. If it had been possible for one of them to be burdened with anxiety or lack, they could trust the other to gladly share in their burden and do whatever was in their means to lift it. They could be careless with one another because they trusted the other would be careful with them.

Though we live in a broken world with fallen people, this kind of trust is available to us. We, too, can experience the precious gift of being able to be *careless* around others because we know they will be careful with us. However, trusting others does come with risk. Once again, even when someone is doing their best to be careful with you, because they are sinful, finite, and weak, they will fall short. Trust always requires some level of faith. But as the seasoned saints say, "It's not the size of your faith that matters. It's the object of it." While these words were crafted to help draw our attention away from the size of our faith to the object of our faith—God—I do believe the principle can also be applied to our relationships.

ESSENTIALS OF TRUST

When taking the step of faith to trust someone, we need to assess the risk. We need to pause and ask ourselves, "Is this person in front of me worthy of my trust? And if so, how much of it?" We need to thoughtfully consider which parts of ourselves we can wisely entrust to them and which parts of ourselves we cannot. Sometimes we may need to invite the counsel of trustworthy others to help us discern the answers to these questions so we can make an informed decision before we extend our trust again.

Dr. Cloud offers these five essentials of trust to look for when trying to discern if someone is worthy of your trust:

1. Understanding.

You can trust someone when you feel your needs are understood, felt, and cared about.

2. Motive.

You can trust someone when you feel their motive is for you, not just for them.

3. Ability.

You can trust someone when you feel they have the ability or capacity to guard and deliver results for what you have entrusted to them.

4. Character.

You can trust someone who has the character or personal makeup needed for what you entrust them with.

5. Track Record.

You can trust someone who has a track record of performing in the ways you need them to perform.[2]

We will revisit Dr. Cloud's five essentials of trust in the following chapters, but for now, I want you to glean the wisdom embedded into this framework: You shouldn't blindly trust anyone. Just like love, trust should fall in the "actions speak louder than words" category. You shouldn't entrust the most precious parts of yourself to someone who has yet to reveal through their words and deeds that they understand and care about you. You should hold off on divulging your personal history until you can discern their motive isn't to manipulatively use that information as leverage to exploit your pain for their personal gain. You need to utilize the gift of time so you can discern if their ability and character make them a good object to put your faith. You should not be careless with someone who has yet to exhibit a track record of being careful with you and others. Emphasis on you *and others.*

Sometimes people are exclusively careful with you because they want something from you. This exclusivity specifically comes up in dating relationships. Your significant other may have a servant's heart toward you but not toward others. They are humble and soft with you but prideful and angry with others. They are available to you but don't have any real friends. These are red flags. As soon as they get what they want from you (sex or marriage), the serving, humble, and soft heart fades, and they suddenly become emotionally or relationally unavailable. I say become, but really, they were all these things all along. They just hid it from you.

Singles, be careful with your heart. Don't get all caught up with three-hour phone calls exchanging personal histories, hopes, and desired futures without first discerning if they can be trusted with these parts of you. "Good morning, beautiful" text messages and dreaming about what your babies will look like is cute. But have they demonstrated in any way that they would make a good partner? A good parent? Are they a person of integrity, or do they always toe the line? Do they possess the ability to tell the truth even when it might put the relationship at risk? Are they wise, or do they often make shortsighted, ill-informed decisions?

Take your time, fam. Give them an opportunity to show you if they are worthy of your trust. And beware of someone who demands it. A trustworthy person who understands the responsibility that comes with being trusted wouldn't feel entitled to it. Instead, they would intentionally engage in the relational work necessary to earn your trust.

JESUS WORKS TO EARN OUR TRUST

Even Jesus does the relational work necessary to earn the world's trust. He comes down from heaven, enters our world, and takes on human flesh to understand the human predicament through the five senses. He doesn't plop down from heaven, and say, "The kingdom of heaven is at hand. Just trust Me," and go back up to heaven. Sure. He starts His ministry saying, "The kingdom of God is at hand; repent and believe," but He follows this command by providing those around Him with evidence that His proclamation is trustworthy, and He is a good place for them to put their faith. Through His teachings and every miracle He performed, He makes an appeal to onlookers to put their trust in Him. He is also so tender and humble with those who are reluctant to put their faith in Him.

When Nathanael, one of Jesus's disciples, initially found it hard to believe that Jesus was the Messiah, Jesus didn't take it personally. It was their first encounter; it was fair for Nathanael not to trust Him. To prove He was worthy of Nathanael's trust, Jesus revealed His divinity. Before Nathanael laid eyes on Jesus, Jesus's eyes were on him. While Nathanael was sitting alone under a fig tree, Jesus—the God Who Sees—saw him (John 1:45-51).

When the Pharisees confronted Jesus for claiming to have the ability to forgive the sins of a lame man, Jesus proved that He indeed possessed the ability to forgive sins by revealing His ability to heal. In response to their distrust, Jesus said to them:

> "Which is easier to say to the paralytic, 'Your sins are forgiven,' or to say, 'Rise, take up your bed and walk'? But that you may know that the Son of Man has authority on the earth to forgive sin"—he said to the paralytic—"I say to you, rise, pick up your bed, and go home" (Mark 2:9-11).

Though the paralytic rose up, picked up his mat, and walked home, the Pharisees persisted in their disbelief. They rejected the evidence presented.

Jesus even made a remarkable amount of relational space for Thomas's struggle to trust. Over the course of three years he had witnessed Jesus heal the sick, cast out demons, cleanse the lepers, and raise the dead. Thomas had even received the power to do the same (Matthew 10:5-8). But when word got to him that Jesus had risen from the dead, he said: "Unless I see in his hands the mark of the nails, and place my finger into the mark of the nails, and place my hand into his side, I will never believe" (John 20:25). There was never a time that he saw Jesus call a demon to come out and it didn't.

At no point did he ever witness Jesus struggle to cause a lame person to walk or bring a dead person to life. Everything Jesus said He would do, He did flawlessly and with ease. But, despite all this evidence, Thomas needed more.

While I want to yell at Thomas, Jesus doesn't. Jesus's response to Thomas's lack of trust is an invitation to inspect and verify His resurrection. He knows that this is what Thomas needs to trust. So He graciously and lovingly says to Thomas: "Put your finger here, and see my hands; and put out your hand, and place it in my side. Do not disbelieve, but believe" (John 20:27). Christ does the relational work to earn Thomas's trust.

Though I don't think we should, like Thomas, persist in demanding more evidence from someone who has already proven themselves to be trustworthy, Thomas's need for more verification reveals to us three things about trust:

1. Trust takes time.

We need to create space for people to show themselves trustworthy and for others to view us the same. My sister-friend, Bree, often jokingly says, "Before I marry somebody, I need to see them in all the seasons twice! I need to see some consistency. I need to know whether or not you are the same person I met last summer or if this summer you're going to present as something different." Though I don't know if I'll be subscribing to this dating method, I've learned to apply the wisdom of taking your time in dating, friendships, joining a church, and even partnering with others in the work of ministry. You need to take the time necessary to become acquainted with the character, values, and patterns of the people you are entrusting yourself to. You need to see how they handle adversity, conflict, and disappointment before you put a ring on it, start calling each other best friends, or embark on a business or ministry endeavor.

2. Trust aptitudes vary from person to person.

In the book of John, we see some people come to trust Jesus quickly and others very slowly. For Andrew, all he needed was for John the Baptist to say, "Behold, the Lamb of God who takes away the sins of the world" to believe Jesus was the Messiah (John 1:35-41). He trusted John the Baptist, so trusting his commendation of Jesus was easy to accept. After one kind, yet convicting conversation with Jesus, the Samaritan woman was so convinced Jesus was the one she and others were waiting on, she ran back to her village to share the good news with everyone (John 4:1-30). Nathanael, on the other hand, needed some more evidence and Thomas, even more.

As you build relationships with others, you need to be aware of your trust aptitude. You need to consider, where is your heart tender and fearful to trust? What past hurts make your runway to trusting people two to three years long? You also need to be aware of the trust aptitude of others. Does the person you are doing life with have past trauma that requires you to be careful around certain triggers so they can be less on guard with you? You need to, like Jesus, be patient with the pace at which others can trust you.

3. Trust should be preceded by inspection.

Like Thomas, we need to look for tactile evidence before we entrust ourselves to others. Even though a new friend or potential boyfriend or girlfriend is hilarious and the two of you share a lot in common, you need to pump the brakes on your feelings to assess the risk. You need to wait until they show some signs that they are trustworthy before moving forward to trust them with the big stuff.

Trust is a gift. It should not be freely or blindly given. Again like love, trust falls in the actions "speak" louder than words category. And as we will see in the next chapter, this is critical to keep in mind when asking the question: Can I trust them—the person who hurt me—again? But before we move forward, let's selah.

SELAH: For this selah, let's meditate on Jesus's encounter with Thomas after His resurrection in John 20:24-28:

> [24] Now Thomas (also known as Didymus), one of the Twelve, was not with the disciples when Jesus came. [25] So the other disciples told him, "We have seen the Lord!" But he said to them, "Unless I see the nail marks in his hands and put my finger where the nails were, and put my hand into his side, I will not believe." [26] A week later his disciples were in the house again, and Thomas was with them. Though the doors were locked, Jesus came and stood among them and said, "Peace be with you!" [27] Then he said to Thomas, "Put your finger here; see my hands. Reach out your hand and put it into my side. Stop doubting and believe." [28] Thomas said to him, "My Lord and my God!"

READ: Read John 20:24-28 slowly and pause over any words or phrases that stand out to you.

REFLECT: Read John 20:24-28 slowly again and pause over Thomas's requirements for belief. Consider all the evidence that he needed to believe and how Jesus was so willing to provide it.

RESPOND: Consider the evidence you need to trust others.

- Of Dr. Cloud's five essentials of trust (understanding, motive, ability, character, and track record), which ones are most important to you?

- What would you say is your "trust aptitude"? Are you slow or fast to trust? Do you need more evidence to trust particular kinds of relationships or circumstances? If so, invite the Holy Spirit to help you understand why.

REST: Take a moment to consider the people in your life who you can be careless with. Rest in the gift of trust you share in those relationships. Consider calling or texting them to thank them for being a trustworthy person in your life.

CHAPTER 15

CAN I TRUST THEM AGAIN?

It bears all things, believes all things,
hopes all things, endures all things.

PAUL, 1 CORINTHIANS 13:7 (csb)

I t's natural to ask this question after an offense. It's also warranted and supremely wise. For so long, I lived under the assumption that forgiveness equaled a full restoration of trust. I even felt guilty if, after making the committed decision to forgive, I still struggled to trust them again. But that was misplaced guilt. When someone has violated our trust, it's appropriate to question whether they can be trusted again. Forgiveness is *the merciful decision to release an offender of a debt and to not retaliate against then in anger.* It's not the decision to reconcile or trust them again. I know they promised not to do it again, but you need to hold off on trusting them until you see some supporting evidence.

Forgiveness, reconciliation, and trust are not all the same. Each have distinct meanings and unique works. They are each different steps in what can be a collaborative process to help move a relationship beyond offense. To help us discern how these steps are different from one another, let's return to Jesus's debt analogy. If an offense is someone making an unauthorized withdrawal that sends your relational account into the red, we can think of forgiveness, reconciliation, and trust in the following ways:

- Forgiveness clears the debt but brings about no change to the relational account. The relational account is still in the red.

- Reconciliation resets the relationship, bringing the relational account out of the red to zero. While there is no relational debt, there also isn't any relational equity.

- Trust is the currency that funds the relational account, restoring safety, security, and shalom in the relationship.

Much of what a relationship looks and feels like in the wake of an offense is determined on how much trust can be restored. After someone sins against you, even if they apologize and state their desire to repent, you are left contending with the question: How *careful* do I need to be moving forward? Again, this line of questioning doesn't reveal a lack of forgiveness or commitment to pursue reconciliation. This line of questioning reveals wisdom. As a result of their offence, you've discovered you can no longer be as *careless* with them as you were before. It is right for you to reassess what's relationally possible moving forward.

However, the amount of trust that can be restored in the relationship isn't solely dependent on the repentance and actions of the offender. Remember, reconciliation is *the committed decision of both the offended and the offender to do the hard work of restoring safety, security, and shalom to the relationship*. Where your offender's work is primarily making deposits into the relational account to help earn your trust, you make deposits into the relational account by verifying the changes they are making and choosing to trust them. They can be doing everything humanly possible and objectively right to earn your trust. But, like Thomas, you can still be wrestling with doubt, needing and maybe even unduly demanding more evidence. The relational account will only be restored if both of you are willing to turn the corner and rebuild trust.

DISCLAIMERS

In this chapter, we will discuss what is the shared but distinct work of both the offender and the offended when it comes to rebuilding trust. But first, a few disclaimers. Before we get too far into this chapter, I want to be careful to shepherd and counsel your expectations. Be careful to not make restoring the relationship to what it was before the goal of rebuilding trust in the relationship. Remember, your relationship has suffered an earthquake.

When the literal earth quakes, "two blocks of the earth suddenly slip past one another."[1] The way the two blocks relate to one another is forever changed. However, in the case of human relationships, this isn't necessarily a bad thing. The offense has revealed a need for change. How you were relating to one another wasn't working and the "slip" necessitates some relational pivots. In many cases, establishing new ways of relating to one another can make the relationship better than it was before. Better, but still different. Don't expect a return to the pre-earthquake reality. It's just not possible.

I have personally seen marriages get significantly better after infidelity and experienced the gift of friendships becoming richer after experiencing the strain of conflict. The love and trust are deeper because each person stayed to do the hard work of forgiveness, reconciliation, and rebuilding trust.

However, I have also witnessed and experienced the pain of relationships seemingly becoming shallower rather than deeper. Instead of feeling like the relationship is moving forward, it bears all the marks of moving backward. You don't laugh as freely. You don't share as much as you did before and neither do they. Your relational rhythms are altogether different. It just feels awkward and you're not sure if it's worth continuing to pursue. Here are two guiding principles that help me move forward when a relationship feels like it's moving backward:

1. Grieve what was lost and accept what's relationally possible.

To give the relationship a fighting chance to live beyond offense, you must name and grieve what was lost and accept what's relationally possible. You need to shift your gaze from the rearview mirror to the open road ahead. If you don't, the relationship is bound to suffer a collision due to persistent discontentment. Don't let your relationship's inability to remain in its former state stifle your ability to explore and enjoy what's relationally possible.

2. Don't confuse intimacy with health.

The two of you may not laugh as hard as you used to, but you also don't fight as much. You sin against one another less. You honor God in the ways you relate to one another more. The new ways you relate to one another have moved the relationship in the direction of health. You may not *feel* as tight as you used to, but the relationship has a better foundation and is no longer in danger of suffering any other big slips. This is a good thing, especially if the relationship was marked by codependency and idolatry. Intimacy fueled by enmeshment and idolatry is not a part of God's relational design.

Unfortunately, these are principles I learned late in life. I often wish I could go back in time to apply them to the relationships that were never given the opportunity to live beyond offense. Maybe some of the intimacy would've been lost but at least we would've been able to maintain some of it. We might not have laughed as hard, but even a shared giggle would've echoed the power of Christ's restorative grace. Sure, the relationship would be different. But what could've happened if both of us stayed present long enough to explore and learn to enjoy what was now relationally possible?

REBUILDING TRUST

In chapter 9 under the guidance of Jesus's teaching in Matthew 18:15-20, we learned reconciliation is impossible apart from the offender's confession and repentance. These two responses are foundational for resetting the relationship and bringing the relational account to zero. However, though the account is no longer in the red, it isn't in the black either. The slate is clean. The possibilities are endless. But what's relationally possible moving forward has yet to be discerned and much of it depends on both parties' ability to do the hard work of rebuilding trust. Let's return our attention to defining what is the shared but distinct work of both the offender and the offended when it comes to rebuilding trust.

The Offender's Work

Using Dr. Cloud's five essentials of trust as a rubric, here are some signs I recommend you look for when trying to discern whether you can trust someone who's hurt you again:

Understanding. The offender needs to show evidence with their words and actions that they understand the impact of their sin against you. Their ability to articulate the pain they've caused and what you need to restore the relationship speaks to their level of awareness about what has happened. Their willingness to be patient with you as you heal and learn to extend trust again reveals their depth of understanding of the pain they've caused. These markers are all good starts that can give you reason for moving toward trusting them again. If they're a Christian, their ability to openly confess their sin against God, grieve, and repent is also a good start. However, it's only a start.

Motive. Though someone can thoughtfully articulate the impact of their offense, this doesn't mean they have trustworthy motives. Instead of primarily seeking to restore trust in the relationship, they are seeking to restore their status within it. Their reason for doing this could be multilayered, but here are a few examples:

- They can't deal with the emotional guilt and shame of hurting you, so they worked hard to stitch together the right words to restore their sense of self-worth.

- They fear that if the relationship fails, it will reflect poorly on them before those whose opinions they revere the most.

- If they can't convince you that it won't happen again, they worry that you will leave them. They don't know how they will manage without your love, partnership in ministry, or financial support.

At the center of each of these motives is the restoration of their shalom, not your shalom or the shalom of the relationship. To discern if their motives are indeed sincere you need to look for evidence that points to them becoming less self-centered and more other-centered. Has their ability to consider you in their decision-making increased? Are they willing to be patient with you while you slowly rebuild trust? What do others say about their motives?

Ability. This one is tough because while someone may understand what they did wrong and have the right motives for wanting to restore trust in the relationship, they may not possess the ability to do what's necessary to do so. It's not that they are unwilling to do the work. They just don't know how to due to their addiction, past trauma, remedial level of self-awareness, or where they are in their sanctification process. They don't yet have the skills and resources they need to repair the kind of damage the two of you are facing. In these unfortunate cases, you will need to grieve what's lost and accept what's relationally possible based on their ability to be *careful* with you.

Character. Is the ethos of their character changing? Are they becoming more humble in the areas they were once prideful? Has their ability to be slow to speak and quick to listen improved? If so, they will be quick to listen, open to reveiving godly counsel, and less defensive when humbly confronted. Did their heart change or just their behavior? If not, they will just find a new venue to house their acts of *self-conscious, self-centered self-preservation.*

Track Record. Though you can't always get under the hood of someone's heart to assess their character, you can assess it based on a proven track record. Behavior modification apart from a real heart transformation will only hold for so long. In time, the behaviors will fade and what resides in the heart will be revealed. But if their behaviors hold and they are steadily moving in the direction of honoring you and glorifying God, you can trust a true resurrection has happened in their heart. They may still mess up, but even then, if they freely confess their sins and recommit to repentance, you have good reason to persevere in continuing to build trust.

The Offended Party's Work

After offense, your primary responsibility is to watch and prayerfully discern how *careless* or *careful* you need to be in the relationship moving forward. Again, forgiveness and reconciliation does not equal a full restoration of trust. Your relational account may now be in good standing, but the balance sits at zero. As your offender makes deposits of understanding their fault and your needs, reveals that their motives are to look out for your interests and not only their own, proves their ability to make good on their resolve to change, grows in godly character, and presents a convincing track record of change, then you have good reason to make deposits of trust. However, it is wise for the pace of your trust to mirror the pace of their change. Though you don't want to unduly withhold trust, you also don't need to blindly extend it. You need to patiently and wisely wait for their desire to restore safety, security, and shalom to the relationship.

When discerning how careless or careful you need to be with someone, here are some red flags to look out for:

1. A shallow apology.

Once again, if they lack an ability to articulate how they have sinned against you and caused you pain, you need to be careful. Their lack of awareness and empathy should give you pause. Statements like, "I'm sorry you feel that way" and "I'll do better next time" paired with distant, dismissive, or apathetic tones are all red flags. But words like "I'm sorry for the pain I've caused" and "It is my desire to change so I can love you in a way that honors God," reveals they have a good level of understanding and that their motives are centered on restoring safety, security, and shalom in the relationship and to you.

2. They don't change; they only pivot.

Their act of self-conscious, self-centered self-preservation doesn't disappear, it merely finds a new home. They may no longer cheat on you, but they withhold information about trivial things. Their high need for autonomy and individualism still leads them to offend, just in new arenas. They no longer gossip about you behind your back, but now they make sly or sarcastic comments to your face. They have yet to learn how to control their anger and present their grievances in a God-honoring way. They are still centering themselves and have only found new ways to inflict pain. The ethos of their character has not changed.

3. An overuse of first-person pronouns.

In his article "Manipulative Repentance: Eight Red Flag Phrases," counselor and pastor Brad Hambrick suggests that we should be concerned when the person repenting uses an "excessive" amount of "self-centered pronouns." Though they should use first person pronouns when taking responsibility for their sin and communicating their resolve to repent, an overuse of first-person pronouns "may reveal that the person is focusing on their personal experience of the offense more than the impact on the person they hurt or offended." They are still selfishly making themselves the "main character" in the relationship.[2]

4. Lack of growing self-awareness.

In her book *Insights*, organizational psychologist and researcher

Tasha Eurich defines internal self-awareness as an "inward under-standing of your values, passions, aspirations, ideal environment, patterns, reactions, and impact on others."[3] A person who lacks this kind of self-awareness is dangerous. I would even argue that some-one who is unaware of why they do what they do—and how what they do impacts others—is more dangerous than a person who is aware. Their lack of internal self-awareness makes them liable to sin against you again.

5. Lack of emotional and spiritual growth.

A person's emotional and spiritual maturity is intricately con-nected to their level of self-awareness. A person can't change what they can't see or are unwilling to see. The offense has revealed there are still places in their heart that have yet to be healed by the trans-formative power of the gospel. However, if they are unwilling to pur-sue healing and transformation by going to counseling, entering a discipleship relationship with someone more mature than them, or spending more time in God's Word, prayer, and fellowship with oth-ers, you need to take note of this and proceed with caution.

For many of us, in the wake of an offense, the last thing we want to do is have to be this *careful.* We just want to get back to the way things were. We crave the intimacy that was lost and want to enjoy it again as soon as possible. But, friend, this is unwise. It neither pro-tects your heart nor causes your offender to grow up and out of the thoughts and behaviors that led to their sin against you. If you reward them with trust too fast, you will rob them of their need to grow. When we are in the thick of conflict with one another, we need to make God's goals our goals. Just as we need to prioritize God's value for relational harmony, we need to prioritize His value for personal sanctification. God's goal isn't only for them to restore their relation-ship with you, but also with Him. And a person living under the conviction of God's Word and His Spirit is more trustworthy than one who is only seeking to get back into your good graces.

While I fall in the camp of extending trust too quickly, I know that some of you reading tend to extend trust more slowly. Possibly even too slowly. Though your friend or significant other has a two-year track record that proves they are worthy of trust, you still need more evidence. If this is you, I encourage you to invite God and others to inspect your heart to discern whether you are struggling to extend trust or willfully withholding it. If you are willfully withholding trust, you could be creatively withholding forgiveness. You are still seeking payment for what they've done. You claim "hurt" is your barrier to trust, but really it's your anger.

However, if you're genuinely struggling to trust even though your offender is showing all the signs of being more trustworthy, you may need more time to heal, a restored confidence in your ability to trust yourself, or a renewed trust in God. If you want the relationship to move forward, you need to be able to identify what your heart needs to be able to trust again and pursue.

Remember, so much of what a relationship looks and feels like in the wake of an offense depends on how much trust can be restored. But the amount of trust that can be restored in the relationship isn't solely dependent on the repentance and growth of the offender. You have to make the hope-filled decision to trust again.

———————————

SELAH: For this selah, let's meditate on Paul's famous love poem in 1 Corinthians 13:4-7:

> [4] Love is patient, love is kind. Love does not envy, is not boastful, is not arrogant, [5] is not rude, is not self-seeking, is not irritable, and does not keep a record of wrongs.

⁶ Love finds no joy in unrighteousness but rejoices in the truth. ⁷ *It bears all things, believes all things, hopes all things, endures all things* (emphasis mine).

READ: Read 1 Corinthians 13:4-7 slowly and pause over any words or phrases that stand out to you.

REFLECT: Read 1 Corinthians 13:4-7 slowly again and pause over verse 7. Consider what it means for you to move forward with your repentant heart, bearing, believing, hoping, and enduring all things. However, keep everything we've discussed so far in this book in mind. Love does not create space for people to continue to sin against us. Remember, love faithfully casts, humbly confronts, and decisively commits. What would it look like for you to apply this kind of love with others?

RESPOND: Consider your relationship with the person who broke your trust.

- Using Dr. Cloud's five essentials of trust (understanding, motive, ability, character, and track record) as a rubric, has the person who sinned against you exhibited any of these qualities? If so, how?

- Given what you've observed, what do you believe is relationally possible moving forward? In what areas or topics of conversation can you be careless with them? In what areas or topics of conversation do you need to remain careful?

REST: Take a moment to consider the people in your life who you can be careless with. Rest in the gift of trust you share in those relationships. Consider calling or texting them to thank them for being a trustworthy person in your life.

CAN I TRUST ANYONE AGAIN?

Two are better than one...if either of them
falls down, one can help the other up.
ECCLESIASTES 4:9-12 (NIV)

When someone breaks our trust, we tend to project their fail- ures onto others. What's unique becomes universal. Truths that should only be localized to a particular person or event becomes a general assumption about all people, everywhere.

My dad's abandonment left me with the chronic feeling of being unwanted. Due to his absence, I have carried a fear of rejection into almost every relationship. Though with time, good counsel- ing, a loving community, and the transformative power of God's Word, the fear has waned, yet it still whispers. I'm thankful God has helped me to grow out of this fear. But, for most of my life, it was like a hum of white noise that went with me everywhere. Always in the background of conversations, causing me to be guarded and turning up its volume if people got too close. "Yana, they will leave you. Don't trust them. Don't fall too deep in love only for them to leave." Like white noise, I couldn't decipher the static to discern where these feelings were coming from. I didn't understand why every time a friendship got good, I would pull back or why when people took an interest in me, I immediately became suspicious. *Surely, they couldn't love me or want to be my friend, mentor, or boyfriend? They must want something else and maybe I should give it to them to make sure they stay.*

In her book, *Why Am I Like This?*, trauma therapist Kobe Campbell writes:

> Our childhood experiences are the very foundation of our understanding of the world we live in. They shape how we perceive ourselves and others, including God. They set the tone for who we believe we are and what we believe we are worthy of. Our childhood trauma affects us more than just psychologically and emotionally; it affects us biologically as well, shifting the way our bodies operate… wiring how our brains interact, which is the foundation of the patterns of our everyday lives.[1]

I wish I had encountered Kobe's wisdom earlier in life. Then, maybe I would've been able to decipher the static to understand how my dad's abandonment was shaping my perception of myself, God, and others. From childhood, his absence developed these three core beliefs: (1) I am unwanted and unlovable; (2) people leave; (3) you must please them if you want them to stay. If I had known this then, maybe I would've been able to quiet my fears enough to bravely be loved. Maybe instead of falling back when relationships got good, I would've leaned in to make them all the richer. Maybe I wouldn't have anxiously worked so hard to get the wrong people to stay. Maybe I would've been better equipped to discern the difference between when I needed to be *careful* with people and when I could enjoy the gift of being *careless*. Maybe I would've sought out the help I needed earlier to rewire my brain so my soul could better give and receive love from God and others.

YOU NEED PEOPLE TO HEAL

Research says, "It takes at least five positive comments to balance one negative" and it can often be much more if the negative "hits deep."[2] If this is what it takes to balance one negative comment, imagine what it takes to balance out the abandonment of a parent, a spouse's repeated infidelity, a betrayal that alters your dreams and hopes, abuse that alters your body chemistry and sense of self-worth, or church hurt that's left your faith hanging on by a thread. How much love, presence, gentleness, care, and understanding does it take to restore someone's sense of safety, security, and shalom in the aftermath of offense? How many positive experiences do we need to help grow out of being *overly careful* with others to become *wisely careless*?

The answers to the questions "how much" and "how many," vary from person to person. For me, it took Lorna Johnson, my first boss in vocational ministry, telling me almost daily over the course of two years that I was loved for me to believe it. It took Moe and Sandy Hafeez opening up their home, letting me eat as often (and as much) as I wanted at their dinner table for me to learn that sometimes people do stay. It took years of reading, studying, meditating on, and praying through Scripture for me to no longer see God through the lens of my earthly father and to believe He would never leave or forsake me. It took the patient and loving friendship of Bree Carnes, LaToya King, and Elizabeth Woodson to heal the wounds of friendship betrayal and loss. It took the good people of Vertical Church to believe that as a Black woman called to preach and teach, I no longer needed to cower myself or my gifts in a corner to appease others. Under their care and constant encouragement, I have learned to be brave and obedient to Christ in all things for His glory and the good of His people. In so many ways, this book wouldn't exist apart from these people and the many others who have done the hard work of convincing me that: (1) I am valued and loved; (2) sometimes people stay; (3) those who require me to please them to stay are unsafe.

Friend, I don't know what it will take for you to grow out of being *overly careful* with others to becoming *wisely careless* after the wounds you have incurred at the hands of others. But what I do know is this: You need people to heal. Your experiences of rejection can only be healed by experiences of acceptance. Your church hurt cannot be healed apart from the loving arms of the church. Only friendships marked by sacrificial love, celebration, and confession can tend to the wounds of those marked by betrayal, competition, and jealousy. You can only know if anyone can be trusted by taking the risk to trust. *You need people to heal.*

Apparently, the clinical term for this phenomenon is *corrective emotional experience*. Let's thank Kobe again for exposing us to language that helps us make sense of our human experience. In her book, which I think you should get, she explains that one of the primary ways we heal is by having positive experiences that "mirror the ways [we] were wounded."[3] You need people who will enter your story and apply love to your wounds in a way that alters the plotline of your narrative. You need people to listen to heal the wounds of not being heard. You need people to be gentle to heal the scars left by those who emotionally and physically abused you. You need people to stay to counter the years of abandonment that taught you that people leave.

Here are five principles that have led me to positive experiences that mirror the ways I've been wounded. Working in tandem with one another, they have taught me that though people are broken and fallen, they are also wildly beautiful, and some of them are undeniably trustworthy.

Make Yourself Available to the Healing Process

In addition to telling me I was loved almost every day, Lorna also repeatedly deposited these borrowed words from Peter Scazzero into my heart: "Yana, 'it is not possible to be spiritually mature while remaining emotionally immature.'"[4] Initially, I heard Lorna's words as a decree of judgment. But for every time she stated these words to me, she affirmed her love for me a hundred times over with her patience, correction, and open invitation to nap on her couch whenever needed. Eventually, I listened to her and tried counseling again with the resolution to understand why I was so guarded yet so needy and how that all connected to my father's abandonment. I also wanted to figure out what I needed to do to be sure my fears of abandonment didn't continue to spill over into my relationships with others.

Nowadays there are a plethora of resources available to help you along your healing journey. For you to move forward in life—beyond offense—you must make yourself available to the healing process. If financial strain isn't the roadblock, you need to stop putting off counseling and go. Then you need to go to counseling and tell the truth. If finances are your greatest barrier, find a podcast hosted by a clinical professional, Christian counselor, or ministry leader who can help you understand your story and the pain associated with it. While you need to be wise about the voices you consume, there are voices you can trust.

Learn to Decode Your White Noise

As you avail yourself to the healing process, you will learn to decode the white noise that hums in the background of your interactions with others and has come to shape your beliefs about God, yourself, and others. This is reflective work, and though it doesn't come naturally to all, it is a skill that can be learned.

With each selah section, I have sought to help you learn this skill. If you skipped over those, I forgive you. I promise to not retaliate in anger against you. However, I encourage you to ask yourself why you skipped sections and why you tend to opt out of reflective moments these altogether. Are you afraid of what the reflective moments will reveal? Do you need the comfort of someone else's presence to help you look long enough at your story to decode your white noise? Have you allowed the mantras "I don't have enough time" or "I have too much stuff to do" to keep you from slowing down to care for your soul?

Friend, your healing needs your time and your attention. Don't you want to be free of the hum of anxiously seeking the approval of others, the need to be successful to prove the naysayers wrong, or the pain your abuser or offender caused? Don't you want to not only be free from the need to retaliate against them, but also free from being controlled by the pain they've caused? If so, you've got to look at what you'd rather avoid and decode the white noise of your story. Much of this starts with asking questions like:

1. When (insert the name of the new person you're building trust with) asked _____, it made me feel _____. Why did it make me _____? Have I felt this feeling before, if so, when and with who?

2. Why do I tend to pull back relationally when people do _____? What am I afraid of? What am I trying to protect?

3. I like _____, but I don't know if I can trust them. Is this concern valid? Is there something about their character that should give me pause or is it that their personality reminds me of someone who hurt me?

In order to decode your white noise, you will need to slow down to ask yourself these questions and others like it. Your soul is worth the cost of investing this kind of time and work to heal. The good people in your life and those who will come are also worth it.

Learn to Separate Your Past from Your Present

I cannot tell you how many times I've had to say to myself: "Yana, this person is not your dad." I was learning to let down my guard and more freely receive and give love, but anytime someone cancelled our plans or took more than five minutes to respond to my text messages my internal alarm system would go off. Was this person safe? Would they leave me too? Should I break up with them before they break up with me?

When an alarm system goes off in someone's home, they get a phone call from their security company. They call to verify if there is indeed a thief in the home or if it's a false alarm. They seek to get clarity from the homeowner before they alert the police.

When our internal alarm system goes off, we need to become skilled at discerning whether there is indeed a thief in our midst. Before we call the authorities (that is, our initial feelings) to remove the person from our lives, we need to ask ourselves: "Is this a false alarm?" The alarm has gone off because someone has brushed up against a part of your story that's still tender, but are they a thief or merely a friend trying to get in. Sure, maybe they should've knocked on the door instead of barging in with such an invasive question. And yes, it's alarming when their personality or style is similar to the person who hurt you. But personality and style are not the same as motives and character. Their relational pace may be faster than yours, making you suspicious and uncomfortable, but are they trying to get in to hurt you or heal you? Is their motive to sincerely know you, not use you?

In the wake of offense, you must learn how to separate your past offender from the people who are presently before you. If you don't, even though you have forgiven your offender, you will make the new person in front of you pay their debt. You may even use the anger stored up in your memory to cause you to retaliate against this new person in the ways you wish you would've done with your offender. This is why you need to heal. This is why you need to decode and understand your white noise. Apart from this work, you will be unable to separate the past from the present and you may end up becoming the offender in someone else's plotline.

Adopt a Biblical Worldview of People

To help untangle your past from your present, you need to adopt a biblical worldview of people. You need a story that exists outside of your story to help you see humanity more comprehensively. Though people are broken and fallen, that's not all that they are or can be. They are people created in the image of God who Christ died for and can be redeemed from the worst of their shortcomings. Though there are some whose lives are marked by self-conscious, self-centered self-preservation, there are an overwhelming number of others who are committed to living out self-giving, other-centered sacrificial love. They are not perfect, but they try. They fall short, but they confess, repent, and are willing to do what it takes to be reconciled. Humanity is not all bad. They're a mix.

If you and I are going live beyond offense to find and enjoy relationships marked by *self-giving, other-centered sacrificial love*, we must abandon our pessimistic or idealistic view of others. We must not allow a low view of humanity to cause us to put the bar so low that we only expect the worst. And we shouldn't put the bar so high that no one but Jesus can reach it. We must accept the truth that we live in a broken world with fallen people, and we must believe that not all broken and fallen people are untrustworthy.

Take Wise Relational Risks

As we make ourselves available to the healing process, learn to decode our white noise, begin the work of separating the past from the present, and come to adopt a biblical worldview of humanity, we are better equipped to take wise relational risks.

These risks don't have to be grand. You don't need to cannonball into any new relationships. As we've already discussed in this section, we should never blindly trust. You can start by sitting on the edge of the pool swapping interests and seeing how they respond when your opinions don't match. Do they ask more questions to understand your point of view, or do they discredit yours in a way that makes you feel inferior? If they seek to *understand*, then you can put your feet in the water by sharing something more personal. It doesn't have to be deep, but something that gives them a window in. See how they respond. Do they listen? Do they exhibit an *ability* to empathize with you in the sad or joyful? Do they shut down or open up in response? If it seems like the water seems fine, get in. Start to do life with one another and get a better sense of their character and values. When your internal alarm system goes off, because it will, check to see if it's a false alarm, if you need to humbly confront, or make your way back to the edge of the pool. You're not leaving; you're just reassessing how *careless* you can be with them moving forward. But if, in time, you can trust that their motives are for you and they have a proven track record to back it up, cannonball in, friend. Enjoy the gift of trust and the healing it can bring.

SELAH: For this selah, let's sit with the truths of why two is better than one in Ecclesiastes 4:9-12 (NIV):

> [9] Two are better than one,
>> because they have a good return for their labor:
> [10] If either of them falls down,
>> one can help the other up.
> But pity anyone who falls
>> and has no one to help them up.
> [11] Also, if two lie down together, they will keep warm.
>> But how can one keep warm alone?
> [12] Though one may be overpowered,
>> two can defend themselves.
> A cord of three strands is not quickly broken.

READ: Read Ecclesiastes 4:9-12 slowly and pause over any words or phrases that stand out to you.

REFLECT: Read Ecclesiastes 4:9-12 slowly again and pause over verse 10. Think of a time in your life when God used you to help someone who had been knocked down by offense get back up again.

RESPOND: Consider any personal barriers you may have to trusting others and potential next steps.

- Is it healing? If so, have you made yourself available to the healing process? If not, what next step can you take? If you have, how is it going and is there anything else you need to heal?

- Is it learning to decode your white noise? If so, how would you describe your white noise? How has this white noise shaped your beliefs about God, self, and others?

- Is it learning how to separate the past from the present? If so, who is one person in your life that you struggle to do this with the most? Take a moment to list out how they may be similar but different from the person who hurt you. Use Dr. Cloud's five essentials of trust (understanding, motive, ability, character, and track record) to discern whether your concerns are false alarms or valid.

REST: Take a moment to consider the people God has brought into your life to mirror the ways you've been wounded. Take a deep breath and rest in the ways they have helped you heal. Give thanks to the Lord for His faithful provision for trustworthy friends for the journey from here to eternity.

CHAPTER 17

CAN I TRUST MYSELF AGAIN?

*Now if any of you lacks wisdom, he should
ask God—who gives to all generously and
ungrudgingly—and it will be given to him.*

JAMES, JAMES 1:5 (csb)

It's possible you blame yourself for what happened. You've played back the footage of the relationship over and over in your mind and concluded if you had not done _____ or had spoken up when they _____, none of this would've happened. Now, you struggle to know if you can trust yourself. Can you make good decisions, or do you have a "bad picker"? Can you trust yourself to not put yourself in harm's way again? Do you know how to identify trustworthy people and build relationships marked by *self-giving, other-centered sacrificial love?*

Though these are fair questions to ask, I want to make something very clear: You are not responsible for someone else's sin. Even if you had led them all the way up to the edge, their decision to jump is theirs to own. To argue differently wouldn't even fly in the court of heaven. If your offender were to suggest to God, "They made me do it" or "I wouldn't have done it if they hadn't made me angry," He wouldn't remove their sin from their ledger and place it on yours. This kind of blame shifting didn't even work for Adam in the garden. Their sin is not your fault.

It's tempting to make it our fault because on some level it restores our sense of control. You can control your decision to change, but you can't control their decision to repent. If you make all of it or some of it your fault, then you're not a victim. You're merely someone who made a bad decision. To say you're a victim means that at some point someone other than yourself had more control over you. But it's no good to regain control by blaming yourself for their sin. For one thing, it's not true. For another, you'll find yourself with less agency and control, not more, if you follow this line of thinking. So hear me again: Their sin is not your responsibility. It's theirs. Your responsibility is to learn from it.

Learning from what happened is an integral step in restoring trust with yourself. In this chapter, I want to help you learn how to trust yourself again by identifying the foreshocks that may have occurred in your relationships with those who have offended you, any unhealthy patterns you need to own and grow out of, and helpful allies for building trust with others moving forward.

IDENTIFYING FORESHOCKS
AND WARNING SIGNS

Prior to an earthquake, there can sometimes be foreshocks. These are smaller earthquakes that precede a larger one. But as researcher and geophysicist Lisa Wald explains, "Scientist can't tell that a [smaller] earthquake is a foreshock until the larger earthquake happens."[1] This can also be true in our relationships. When the earthquake took place in your relationship, it's possible there were some foreshocks. Not all earthquakes have foreshocks, but some do.

If you were to play back the tape on your relationships with the people who offended you, would you find any foreshocks? Were there any statements, behaviors, or the lack thereof that you think could've contributed to the offense? Were there any minor offenses that were easier to forgive that led to a major one that made the relationship no longer bearable? When you look back on the terrain of your relationship, what do you see?

Now, as you look back, avoid the temptation to blame yourself. Remember, their sin is their responsibility, not yours. We don't replay the tape to blame. We replay the tape to learn. Plus, sometimes foreshocks are difficult to see when the relationship is mostly good. You didn't expect them to hurt you because there was so much evidence that they loved you. The foreshock was hard to see. But given what you know now, were there any foreshocks in the relationship that can now be counted as warning signs moving forward? Fill in the chart below.

Foreshock	Warning Signs
Example: They dismissed my feelings and opinions often.	A person who dismisses my feelings and opinions regularly

IDENTIFYING UNHEALTHY PATTERNS

Though we are never responsible for someone else's sin, we must identify any unhealthy patterns we exhibited in the relationship that contributed to its dynamic. As licensed clinical social worker and relationship expert Leslie Vernick explains in her book *The Emotionally Destructive Relationship* to "breathe any health" back into a relationship after an offense "both parties need to make significant changes."[2] Both parties might not be at fault. But both parties need to identify how their thoughts, behaviors, and white noise contributed to the dynamic in the relationship.

As I've played the tape back on the sudden end to my friendship with my non-seasonal friend, I've had to ask the question: How did I contribute to our relationship's dynamic? Without taking ownership for her part in the relationship, I needed to take ownership of mine. I have to own the times I didn't speak up out of fear of being rejected. I must admit how I allowed my fear of abandonment to lead me to over-function, taking on most of the responsibility to hang out or reconcile. I even must accept that my needy, anxious attachment style had suffocated some of the joy out of the relationship. That's my part. And it's on me to continue to make myself available to the healing, decode my white noise, and separate the past from the present to grow out of my unhealthy patterns so they don't negatively impact my relationships moving forward.

When you play back the tape on your relationship with your offender, what unhealthy patterns do you see? Was there ever a time when you needed to humbly confront but didn't? Can you think of any moments when you felt uncomfortable about something but ignored it? If so, use the chart below to write out your unhealthy patterns and then consider opportunities for growth moving forward.

Unhealthy Patterns	Opportunities for Growth
Example: When they dismissed my feelings, I didn't say anything even though I was upset.	Humbly confront others when their words or actions appear dismissive to get clarity on their intent and communicate what you need moving forward

IDENTIFYING HELPFUL ALLIES

When Christ ascended into the heavens, He left us with three gifts: (1) His Word; (2) His Spirit; (3) His people. As we are trying to discern whether or not we can trust our judgment, we need to utilize these three gifts Jesus so graciously provides. We need to lean into His Word, trust His Spirit, and consult His people.

Lean into His Word

In God's Word, we find the truths that we need to live in a broken world with fallen people. In its pages, we encounter stories of human relationships, proverbs of wisdom, and a host of "one another" commands that provide us with counsel for how to treat one another. Through the life of Jesus, we receive the blueprint for how we are to live as shalom-makers. However, these truths, counsel, and blueprint not only put before us a life we are called to live but also provide us with a measure by which we can identify people we can trust.

They may not be perfect, but do they show signs that they share the ethics of Christ's Kingdom? They might not even be a Christian, but do they have a track record of telling the truth, loving others sacrificially, and being aware of their own white noise? Does their character track record give you the ability to be careless with them? Do they confess and repent when they are humbly confronted? If so, these are people worth giving a shot. These are people worth trusting. Allow God's Word to be the rubric by which you measure someone's character. You might feel as though you can't trust your own judgment, but you can always trust His.

Trust His Spirit

There's your gut, and then there's the Holy Spirit. The two are not the same, and the two do not always agree. Your gut is often informed by your past positive and negative experiences, familial upbringing, geographical location, favorite preacher or social media influencer, and white noise. The Spirit, on the other hand, exists in a triune relationship with God the Father and Christ His Son and never wavers from the counsel of God's Word. While your gut may have valuable information to consider, it may not always live in agreement with the Spirit. Your gut may set off your internal alarm system, telling you to run and abort the relationship. But the Spirit may encourage you to stay and get curious. Is it their character or your past that set off the alarm? Your gut might cause you to think that even though it's apparent that the other person has a lot of white noise they need to do the hard work to decode, you can take it. In fact, not only can you take it, but you can fix them. But the Spirit in partnership with God's Word says: "Bear one another's burdens and so fulfill the law of Christ…But let each one test his own work…For each will have to bear his own load" (Galatians 6:2-5). Decoding their white noise is their load. Not yours.

Here's the principle: Consult your gut, trust the Spirit. Again, your gut has valuable information to offer. Consult it. Ask questions. See if it's a false alarm or if you're in danger. However, be mindful that your gut is fallible and can sometimes lead you down crooked paths. The Spirit, on the other hand, is infallible. Trust Him. Even when your gut disagrees. He will always make your path straight (Proverbs 3:5-6).

Depending on where you are in your walk with the Lord or your church background, trusting the Spirit either sounds like a foreign concept or altogether spooky. You may have questions about how to discern His inaudible voice or leading. Like, do I know it's Him when I get a rush of feeling radiating through my body or when I get a nagging impulse to do or not do something? As someone who grew up Pentecostal, got saved in a Presbyterian context, was theologically trained at a Baptist seminary, and now serves at a nondenominational church, I get the question. It can be confusing. Here are three ways to grow in discerning the Spirit's leading:

1. Pray.

In James 1:5, we are instructed to ask for wisdom when we lack it and promised that God will generously give it to all who ask. In faith, ask God to teach you how to listen for and respond to His Spirit that dwells within. Pray, knowing that just as a good father gives good gifts to his children, so does your heavenly Father. He delights to give the Spirit to all who ask. Jesus wants you to know how to respond to the Spirit. It's for this very reason He's given the Spirit to you. He will more than honor your request and will do so with joy.

2. Practice.

If you're like me, you may have a strong desire to get discerning the Spirit's leading just right every time. However, sometimes you will mistake your gut for the Spirit. We don't possess the ability to be perfect, but we do possess the ability to learn. When the Spirit moves you to move in one direction or another, and it's confirmed through your obedience that you discerned Him correctly, make note of it. When it's confirmed that you discerned incorrectly, don't fret. You still belong to God, and the Lord sees you faithfully trying to obey Him. Learn from it and keep practicing. However, be careful to not interpret pleasant or unpleasant circumstances as whether or not the Spirit is leading you. Sometimes, He does lead us into adverse experiences to grow our faith and trust in Him. Trust the process of being able to discern this as well. He will teach you.

3. Inspect.

When trying to discern if the Spirit is leading you, be ever mindful of your heart and its idols. Sometimes that strong rush of emotions is your flesh crying out for comfort, power, or certainty. When you're having trouble deciphering if it's your idols or the Spirit leading you, sit with Psalm 139:23-24. Selah—pause to invite the Spirit to search your heart and test your thoughts. Let Him inspect your heart to reveal any grievous or idolatrous way within you. Then wait and trust Him to lead you in the way everlasting.

There is a bit of a learning curve here, but lean on the other two gifts Jesus has given you to discern when the Spirit is seeking to lead you in one direction or another. The Spirit never contradicts the Word He inspired, and His counsel can be found in a cohort of Spirit-filled believers.

Consult His People

When having difficulty discerning whether or not to trust someone, you can also utilize the gift of God's people. Like your gut, they are fallible. But they also have helpful information and wisdom to offer. If you have people in your life who are familiar with your white noise and have proven themselves to be trustworthy, invite them in to help you separate your past from your present. Invite them to hold you accountable to grow out of your unhealthy patterns in relationships. If you're dating someone new, don't wait too long to bring your people in. And if the person you're dating is resistant to the idea of meeting your family and friends, pay attention to that. If it's their desire to keep people out of y'all's business, that's a red flag. Why does any of y'all's business need to happen in secret or isolation?

If you don't feel like you have people in your life that you can trust, I hope that is more of a feeling than your reality. We all need people in our lives that we can trust. Your next step is to find people you can trust, practicing some of the principles shared in this section. If counseling is an option, start practicing trust there and invite your counselor to help you make decisions about who to trust and how much.

Beloved, you can learn how to trust yourself again. I know that sometimes the offense of others sets off an earthquake not only in the relationship, but in our very souls. We no longer feel the sense of safety, security, and shalom we once shared in the relationship or within ourselves. However, I want you to know that you are not stuck. You can restore the trust you once had with yourself. You can learn from your past foreshocks and use them as warning signs moving forward. You can use the past to protect yourself moving forward. You can grow out of your unhealthy relational patterns and start new relationships on a healthier footing. When reconciliation is possible, you are also capable of staying, setting boundaries, and discerning when to offer trust and how much. God has given you a mind and the ability to make wise decisions. You can trust yourself again.

SELAH: For this selah, let's sit with James's teaching on wisdom in James 1:5 and Jesus's teaching on prayer in Luke 11:9-13:

> [5] If any of you lacks wisdom, let him ask God, who gives generously to all without reproach, and it will be given him (James 1:5).

> [9] And I tell you, ask, and it will be given to you; seek, and you will find; knock, and it will be opened to you. [10] For everyone who asks receives, and the one who seeks finds, and to the one who knocks it will be opened. [11] What father among you, if his son asks for a fish, will instead of a fish give him a serpent; [12] or if he asks for an egg, will give him a scorpion? [13] If you then, who are evil, know how to give good gifts to your children, how much more will the heavenly Father give the Holy Spirit to those who ask him! (Luke 11:9-13).

READ: Read James 1:5 and Luke 11:9-13 slowly and pause over any words or phrases that stand out to you.

REFLECT: Read James 1:5 and Luke 11:9-13 slowly again. Give thanks to God for His willingness to give wisdom and the gift of His Spirit to all who ask.

RESPOND: Ask the Spirit to give you wisdom to discern any foreshocks or unhealthy patterns in your previous relationships with those who sinned against you.

- Go back to your Foreshock and Warning Signs chart. What's one guiding principle or boundary you want to create and adopt for your relationships moving forward?

- Go back to your Unhealthy Patterns chart. Where do you sense you need to grow the most? Who can you invite or what can you do to help you grow in this area?

REST: Ask God to give you the wisdom you need to move forward in your relationships, paying attention to the warning signs and growing out of unhealthy patterns. Ask Him and rest. Trust He will be faithful to His promise to generously give you wisdom.

CHAPTER 18

CAN I TRUST
GOD AGAIN?

*O Israel, hope in the LORD! For with the LORD there is
steadfast love, and with him is plentiful redemption.*

PSALM 130:7

After another stint of prolonged absence, he called. It had been
two years since I heard his voice. But I wasn't sure if I wanted to
hear it. The last time I saw him, he was too drunk, high, and enamored with his new girlfriend to hold a conversation. Plus, during his
absent stint, I had come to terms with the distance in our relationship. I had come to accept that I live in a broken world with fallen
people. I had lamented the tears, cracks, and breaks in my shalom
due to his absence. I had come to understand forgiveness is the merciful decision to release your offender from their debt and not retaliate against them, not forgetting, ignoring, or forcing my feelings
to change.

Instead, I was living with my feelings, decisively committing
to forgive my dad and faithfully casting his forgiven sins into the
depths of the sea when my memory would drift to the pain of his
absence and how it was inhibiting my ability to move forward with
the trusted others before me. God was healing me. He had put people in my life to mirror the pain of my father's absence and provided
me with the opportunity to get the support of good counselors. It

wasn't perfect or easy, but I could sense God changing me, softening my heart so that compassion and mercy would flow. My lead emotion toward my dad was shifting from anger to grief, from frustration to love. So I picked up.

He sounded different. His words weren't slurred. For the first time, in a long time, I heard his sober voice. I also heard his repentant one. He didn't necessarily apologize, that came a few years later, but I could tell he was trying to connect. It was Valentine's Day, and he just wanted to say hello. I chuckled a bit to myself that he skipped over Thanksgiving, Christmas, and New Year's to make this holiday his grand reentrance. But it was so providential that he did.

That morning, I had decided to treat myself to breakfast. Totally unaware that it was Valentine's Day, I scooched into a booth, took out my journal and Bible, and started my devotion. Midway through I looked up and saw table after table filled with what I longed for—a bunch of dads being dads. I'm not over exaggerating when I say this restaurant was filled with dads loving on their kids. I wept. I asked for the check and got out of there as soon as I could. Then, he called.

The phone call was short and afterward I felt very unsure how to move forward, but it was clear to me that God was moving, just as He did before, to let me know that He sees me and He cares. And I know this sounds very fairy-tale-like, but please know that if forgiving my dad was hard, reconciling and learning to trust him was even harder. It was one thing to *faithfully cast* his forgiven sin into the depths of the sea when he wasn't present and a whole thing to do it when standing right in front of me. I had to work hard to separate the past from the present. In the past, he was a no-call, no-show kind of dad. In the present he was calling and apologizing for needing to cancel. In the past, he didn't show up because he was drunk. In the present, he wasn't able to show up because he was a self-employed mechanic taking every job he could to make ends meet. His track record was changing. He was more consistent. Calling too much like most parents to talk about the weather, ask me how my car was running, and giving me advice I didn't ask for. To be honest, it was overwhelming. On the one hand, I was thankful to have him more consistently in my life. But, on the other hand, I had gotten so used to living without him that it was hard to make space for him. However, this wasn't only a matter of fitting time in my schedule, it was also a matter of creating space in my heart. I wasn't sure my heart could take it if he relapsed and went missing again.

I can't remember who said it, but someone in my relational orbit sowed these words into my heart to help steady my fears and silence my what-ifs: "Our ability to trust others is rooted in our ability to trust God. You don't know if you can trust them, but you know you can trust God." Now, I want to sow these words into yours.

TRUSTING GOD

Beloved, your ability to trust others is rooted in your ability to trust God. You may not know if you can trust others, but you can always be assured that you can trust God. As we've already established, we live in a broken world with fallen people who despite their best efforts will disappoint and fail us. Only the God who is holy, holy, holy, can be trusted. Only the God who is infinitely wise and good and loves you with an infinite love can be trusted without fear or hesitation. Only in His arms can you be assured you are safe. He understands your longing for shalom. His motives toward you are to shower you with self-giving, other-centered sacrificial love. Nothing about Him is self-conscious or self-centered. His desire is to preserve you and your faith—not Himself. He possesses the ability to make good on every one of His promises. His character is impeccable, and His track record is solid. But to help assure you of this even more, let's do a quick survey of why we can trust God, using Dr. Cloud's five essentials of trust once more.

Understanding

God longs for shalom with you. His heart breaks every time someone created in His image sins against another image-bearer. Like a parent whose heart is stretched with grief when their children don't get along, His heart is stretched with grief and aches as well. He has witnessed every offense that has ever happened under the sun. He understands the pain of being sinned against. He's acquainted with the pain of seeing someone you love suffer offense. However, remember, He doesn't just sit above it as a grieved witness. In the person of Jesus Christ, He wraps Himself in our weakness and becomes intimately attuned with the hardships and sufferings that come with living in a broken world. He allowed fallen people to betray, abandon, mock, and abuse Him for our salvation and so that He could sympathize with the human experience in every way. Hebrews 4:15-16 (KJV):

> For we have not an high priest which cannot be touched with the feeling of our infirmities; but was in all points tempted as we are, yet without sin. Let us therefore come boldly unto the throne of grace, that we may obtain mercy and find grace to help in time of need.

Beloved, you can trust Him because, in His divinity and humanity, He understands comprehensively the pain of offense. You can go to Him boldly for help, trusting He will help you to navigate the terrain of living in a fallen and broken world as His shalom-maker.

Motive

John 10:10, some of the most honest words in the Bible, says: "The thief comes only to steal and kill and destroy. I came that they may have life and have it abundantly." Though the evil one is roaming over the earth seeking to do harm, Jesus is not. His motives toward you are pure. His command to make the merciful decision to release your offender from their debt and not retaliate against them is for your good. The evil one's suggestion to tighten your grip around their neck and retaliate against them is not. Remember, God doesn't command you to forgive because it serves His redemptive bottom line. He commands you to forgive because unforgiveness and bitterness will erode your heart in ways that will stifle your ability to love and be loved. All of His commands are wrapped up in His mission to give you abundant life. You can be assured that all of His path leads to life. He loves you with an extraordinary love.

Ability

When my dad came back, trusting God's ability to keep me emotionally safe was my biggest challenge. I had done so much work in counseling to heal and grow out of unhealthy thought patterns, coping mechanism, and behaviors. And in the initial years of reconnecting with my father, I fought hard to protect myself. However, in protecting myself from his potential to do harm, I was also shielding myself from his love. But a good friend of mine, Lindsay Lewis, helped me to see that in being so intent on protecting myself and not being open or vulnerable with my dad in any way was false reconciliation.

Sitting with this truth, I realized that to take the next step in living beyond offense in my relationship with my dad I needed to take the risk of trusting my dad again. I also needed to let go of my expectation for God to keep me completely safe from emotional disappointment or harm. This expectation of God this side of heaven didn't par well with the reality of living in a broken world with fallen people. So, instead of trying to lay hold of a promise that would only be possible in the future, I grabbed hold of one I could count on in the present and it's this: Even if my dad hurts me again, God will heal me again.

In this world, we will be disappointed and hurt again. Even when we've made the grand journey of forgiveness once in our lives, we will be met with opportunities to take the journey again. And the unfortunate truth is that sometimes we will have to take the journey as an offender, not the offended. Offense will happen. However, when it does happen, we can trust God's ability to cause our justice and our righteousness to shine like the noonday sun. We can rest and trust in His ability to heal us again, restoring our shalom and causing our body, mind, and soul to thrive again. We can hope in Him because as Psalm 130:7 says, "With the LORD there is steadfast love, and with him is plentiful redemption." He's the God of redemption, and He is not short on resurrection power. He brings life to all fallen and broken things.

Character

In so many ways, the suffering of this world causes us to question whether God is good. But as we established in chapter 13, the problem of evil exists not because there is a problem with God but because there is a problem with humanity. Our God is good. And we find His benevolent heart and glorious character on full display in the bookends of our Bible apart from the presence of sin.

However, as pastor Dane C. Ortlund explains in *Gentle and Lowly*, "The fall of Genesis 3 not only sent us into condemnation and exile. The fall also entrenched in our minds dark thoughts of God." I'm wholeheartedly convinced that this was Satan's goal all along. All throughout Scripture, he wills suffering, abuse, and offense into the lives of the biblical characters to cause their faith to slip. If his mission statement is to kill, steal, and destroy us, his sole strategy is to use others to bring suffering and the fires of hell into our lives to extinguish our faith. It's for this reason Ortlund adds: "[these dark thoughts of God] are only dug out over multiple exposures to the gospel over many years."[1]

Beloved, fight for faith—faith in God's goodness, His just character, and His enduring love for you. Fan the flame of your faith by meditating often on the gospel and character of God laid out for you in Scripture. Don't let the evil one and the suffering he wills in your life through fallen people extinguish your faith. Fight, beloved. Fight. Keeping God's impeccable character and track record in view.

Track Record

When you look back over your life, what do you see? Where do you see God's hand at work in you, around you, and for you? What's His track record?

When I look back over my life, though I see a couple of friendships that have dissolved or shifted, I see so many more that didn't. God's hand has been at work in me, around me, and for me. He used the grief of lost friendships to reveal my idols and areas of my heart that still needed to be healed. He's made 20-year-old friendships richer and put new people around me who have shown themselves to be worthy of trust. I know they say it's harder to make friends when you're older, but it's been such a joy to do life with a bunch of healed people. It's been a gift. It's also been such a sweet gift for Him to bring old friends back.

Now, every time He brings a new friend into my life and I want to shrink back, I remind myself of God's track record to lead me to the right people and to heal me when I get hurt. He's been faithful, and His faithfulness will continue.

Beloved, you can trust Him.

SELAH: In this final selah, I want to invite you to sit with the words I have mediated on almost every day of writing this book in Psalm 131.

> [1] O LORD, my heart is not lifted up;
>   my eyes are not raised too high;
> I do not occupy myself with things
>   too great and too marvelous for me.

² But I have calmed and quieted my soul,
    like a weaned child with its mother;
    like a weaned child is my soul within me.
³ O Israel, hope in the LORD
    from this time forth and forevermore.

READ: Read Psalm 131 slowly and pause over any words or phrases that stand out to you.

REFLECT: Read Psalm 131 slowly again. Consider how trusting God is hard for those who occupy themselves with thoughts too great and too marvelous for them.

RESPOND: Read Psalm 131 slowly again.

- When it comes to trusting God, yourself, others, and your offender again, how is your preoccupation with the future and what-ifs hindering your ability to trust?

- What truths about God's understanding, motives, ability, character, and track record do you need to mediate on to calm and quiet your soul?

REST: Read Psalm 131:3 again. Consider all the beautiful reasons why you can hope in the Lord and rest.

CONCLUSION

I did not want to write this book. I sent Harvest House five other book proposals to consider, and in our preliminary meetings, we discussed two or three other ideas. But somehow in our "let's put a ring on it" meeting with the executive leadership team, we started talking about forgiveness. After a few minutes of sharing what God had been teaching me over the past few years through church hurt, friendship loss, and my relationship with my dad, all the heads in their respective Zoom squares nodded in agreement that this was the book.

When we all said our goodbyes, I was initially overwhelmed with excitement. I called my mom and friends who were praying for the meeting to share the good news. By God's incredible kindness and grace, I was on the cusp of signing a book deal. However, as the phone calls ended and the idea of writing a book on forgiveness began to settle in, I started to wonder if I was the girl for the job. Sure, I had some good thoughts about forgiveness and had a story or two to tell. But I could think of at least five people who would laugh out loud at the idea of me writing a book on forgiveness. Even though I knew that forgiveness didn't equal reconciliation, I started to doubt whether I had really forgiven the handful of people who I wasn't able to fully reconcile with after offense. Could I really write a book on forgiveness? And even if I could, should I, given the broken relationships in my life?

Unsure of the answer to both of those questions, I ghosted Harvest

House. Like Jonah, I ran in the other direction, even though it was clear this was the book Jesus was inviting me to trust Him to write it. Thankfully, Audrey Greeson, my brilliant and ever hopeful editor, reached out to see how my chapter summaries were going. Though I was ready to reply with an email stating I had changed my mind, I felt compelled to take the weekend to pray.

Over the course of the weekend, God revealed that fear was at the core of my stalling. But this wasn't primarily regarding my ability to write the book, but my ability to bear the emotional pain and the sanctifying process that would come with doing so. I knew that if I wrote a book on forgiveness, I would have to go back to moments of pain in my life that God had healed through His love, His Word, and His people. I understood that if I spent hours and hours in God's Word reading and wrestling with Jesus's teaching on forgiveness that God would read and wrestle with me. I was aware that writing this book would not only take me to places in my past I didn't want to go but also lead me to go back to those I had cancelled. It was crystal clear to me that if I wrote this book, I would have to live it. I would be accountable to live up to the new insights and convictions I would attain.

Beloved, I pray over the course of reading this book you've gained new understanding and convictions that help you embrace living in a broken world with fallen people. I hope that knowing you were created for shalom comforts you as you navigate the pain of offense and broken relationship. However, I also hope this truth inspires you to live in God's world as a shalom-maker. This is the role you and I have been cast to play in God's unfolding story.

As we wait for His return, we are to cast aside the *shalom-avoidant* and *shalom-demanding* ways of this world and take up the *shalom-making* ways of Christ and His Kingdom. We are to, like Jesus, seek to fill every tear, crack, and break in this world with His shalom. At times, this call to shalom-making will mean sacrificially loving our neighbor. At other times it will mean sacrificially loving our enemies. It will require us to *decisively commit* to forgive and *humbly confront* those who sin against us, and to *faithfully cast* their forgiven sin back into the depths of the sea when our anger draws up their offense again. It will necessitate us rolling up our sleeves to the merciful decision to release an offender of their debt and to not retaliate against them in anger when everything in you protests it and pursuing reconciliation when possible.

As we come to the end of this book, here is my charge: Forgive as you've been forgiven. Readily extend to others the mercy you've received. Live up to the truths you, by God's grace, have attained through this book. Resolve to live beyond offense. Take up your role to live as God's shalom-maker in this broken world with fallen people.

Blessed are the shalom-makers, for they shall be called the children of God.

Selah.

NOTES

INTRODUCTION

1. Justin Parent, et al., "The Role of Coparents in African American Single-Mother Families: The Indirect Effect of Coparent Identity on Youth Psychosocial Adjustment," *Journal of Family Psychology* 27, no. 2 (2013): 252-262, doi: 10.1037/a0031477.

2. Pricelis Dominguez, "Contemplative Practices," Full Collective, email newsletter, February 26, 2025. Emphasis original.

PART 1: WE LIVE IN A STORY

1. Charaia Rush, *Courageously Soft: Daring to Keep a Tender Heart in a Tough World* (Baker Books, 2024), 10.

CHAPTER 1: A TRUTH WE MUST ACCEPT

1. Kobe Campbell, "Rupture + Repair: The Heart of Every Meaningful Relationship," For Your Journey, February 26, 2025, https://kobecampbell.substack.com/p/rupture-and-repair.

CHAPTER 2: BLESSED ARE THE SHALOM-MAKERS

1. Dan B. Allender and Tremper Longman, *The Cry of the Soul: How Our Emotions Reveal Our Deepest Questions About God* (Colorado Springs: NavPress, 1994), 86-87.

2. John Collins and Michelle Jones, hosts, *BibleProject Podcast*, episode 7, "What Does it Mean to Make Peace? (The Beatitudes Pt. 4)," Sermon on the Mount, joined by Tim Mackie, February 12, 2024, https://open.spotify.com/episode/0MsyIwTe7DkBuSvXfyrh36?si=r_sx3FvAS0-fted HmwocKQ&context=spotify%3Ashow%3A6f2oD3RtQYlrOeyfF2OeOa.

PART 2: WHAT IS FORGIVENESS ANYWAY?

1. Jennifer Berry Hawes, *Grace Will Lead Us Home: The Charleston Church Massacre and the Hard, Inspiring Journey to Forgiveness* (St. Martin's Press, 2019), 74.

2. Ben Brumfield, "Charleston Church Shooting: 9 Killed in South Carolina," CNN, June 26, 2015, https://www.cnn.com/2015/06/26/us/charleston-church-shooting-main/index.html.

3. Hawes, *Grace Will Lead Us Home*, 75.

CHAPTER 3: FORGIVENESS IS A MERCIFUL DECISION

1. Charles L. Quarles, *Matthew*, eds. T. Desmond Alexander, Thomas R. Schreiner, and Andreas J. Köstenberger, Evangelical Biblical Theology Commentary (Lexham Academic, 2022), 466.

2. Quarles, *Matthew*, 468.

3. R.T. France, *The Gospel of Matthew*, The New International Commentary on the New Testament (Eerdmans, 2007), 703-705.

4. James Swanson, *Dictionary of Biblical Languages with Semantic Domains: Greek (New Testament)* (Logos Research Systems, Inc., 1997).

5. Swanson, *Dictionary of Biblical Languages with Semantic Domains.*

CHAPTER 4: THE HARD WORK OF FORGIVENESS

1. Melissa B. Kruger, *The Envy of Eve: Finding Contentment in a Covetous World* (Christian Focus: 2012), Kindle Edition.

2. Hawes, *Grace Will Lead Us Home*, Kindle edition.

CHAPTER 6: FORGIVENESS IS NOT IGNORING

1. Swanson, *Dictionary of Biblical Languages with Semantic.*

2. Quarles, *Matthew*, 180.

3. Quarles, *Matthew*, 180.

4. John Collins and Michelle Jones, hosts, *BibleProject Podcast*, episode 15, "What Jesus Means by 'Turn the Other Cheek,'" Sermon on the Mount, joined by Tim Mackie, April 8, 2024, https://bibleproject.com/podcast/what-jesus-means-turn-other-cheek/.

CHAPTER 7: FORGIVENESS IS NOT A FEELING

1. Jennifer S. Lerner, Ye Li, Piercarlo Valdesolo, and Karim S. Kassam, "Emotion and Decision Making," Annual Review of Psychology 66 (2015): 799–823, https://scholar.harvard.edu/files/jenniferlerner/files/emotion_and_decision_making.pdf.

2. Lerner, et al., "Emotion and Decision Making."

3. Jean M. Twenge, *Generations: The Real Differences Between Gen Z, Millennials, Gen X, Boomers, and Silents—and What They Mean for America's Future* (Atria, 2023), 9-10, Kindle edition.

4. Twenge, *Generations*, 9-10, Kindle edition.

5. Karl Moore, *Generation Why: How Boomers Can Lead and Learn from Millennials and Gen Z* (McGill-Queen's University Press, 2023), 69.

6. J. Alasdair Groves and Winston T. Smith, *Untangling Emotions* (Crossway, 2019), 32-38.

7. Swanson, *Dictionary of Biblical Languages with Semantic Domains.*

CHAPTER 8: JESUS, JUDAS, AND CANCEL CULTURE

1. Clyde McGrady, "The Strange Journey of 'Cancel' from a Black-Culture Punchline to a White-Grievance Watchword," *The Washington Post*, April 2, 2021, https://www.washingtonpost.com/

lifestyle/cancel-culture-background-black-culture-white-grievance/2021/04/01/2e42e4fe-8b24
-11eb-aff6-4f720ca2d479_story.html.

2. "Peace: How Can I Find Inner Peace in a Turbulent World?" panel discussion with Lisa Fields, Charles Goodman Jr., Nicole Massie Martin, and Robert Smith at Courageous Conversations 2024 National Gathering, Washington D.C., August 29-31, 2024.

3. Evan Marbury, *Understanding Trauma and Resilience: A Guide for Counselors, Caregivers, and Ministers* (Baker Academic, forthcoming March 2026).

4. Marbury, *Understanding Trauma and Resilience.*

CHAPTER 9: FORGIVENESS DOESN'T EQUAL RECONCILIATION

1. Emily P. Freeman, host, *The Next Right Thing*, podcast, episode 183, "Real Talk About Over-functioning," September 20, 2022, https://emilypfreeman.com/podcast/183.

2. Swanson, *Dictionary of Biblical Languages with Semantic Domains.*

3. Quarles, *Matthew*, 463.

CHAPTER 10: THE UNFORTUNATE TRUTH

1. John Bevere, *The Bait of Satan: Living Free from the Deadly Trap of Offense* (Charisma House, 2004), 7.

2. Melissa B. Kruger, *The Envy of Eve: Finding Contentment in a Covetous World* (Christian Focus, 2012), Kindle edition.

CHAPTER 11: FORGIVENESS AS A SPIRITUAL DISCIPLINE

1. France, *The Gospel of Matthew*, 242.

2. Ryan Brooks, "Jump to Clarity," sermon, October 18, 2021, Vertical Church, YouTube, https://youtu.be/j25OBc42_lU?si=C9Y_s2PcFpDjREXF.

PART 4: WHEN IT HURTS SO BAD

1. Rahel Naef, "Bearing Witness: A Moral Way of Engaging in the Nurse-Person Relationship," *Nursing Science Quarterly* 19, no. 4 (2006): 313–316, doi: 10.1111/j.1466-769X.2006.00271.x.

CHAPTER 12: LIVING BEYOND ANGER

1. Groves and Smith, *Untangling Emotions*, 170.

2. Swanson, *Dictionary of Biblical Languages with Semantic Domains.*

3. Peter C. Craigie, Psalms 1–50, vol. 19, Word Biblical Commentary (Word Books, 1983), 297.

4. Chris Pappalardo, comment on manuscript, February 21, 2025, used with permission.

CHAPTER 13: LIVING BEYOND ABUSE

1. These psalms that I've referred to as "angry-filled" responses to offense are more formally classified as imprecatory psalms. There are twenty-two of them in our Bibles. Here is the list: Psalm 5, 6, 11, 12, 35, 37, 40, 52, 54, 55, 56, 57, 58, 69, 79, 83, 94, 109, 137, 139, and 143.

2. Christian White, "Balancing Competency and Character," Future Leader Cohort, Summit Collaborative, Atlanta, GA, September 13, 2024.

3. "Protection: Why Didn't God Protect Me?" panel discussion with Christina Edmondson, Esau McCaulley, Brianna Parker, and Phillip Pointer at Courageous Conversations 2024 National Gathering, Washington D.C., August 29-31, 2024.

4. Christina Edmondson, "Protection: Why Didn't God Protect Me?" panel discussion with Christina Edmondson, Esau McCaulley, Brianna Parker, and Phillip Pointer at Courageous Conversations 2024 National Gathering, Washington D.C., August 29-31, 2024.

5. Groves and Smith, *Untangling Emotions*, 169.

6. Chris Pappalardo, comment on manuscript, February 21, 2025, used with permission.

PART 5: TRUSTING AGAIN

1. Mira Kirshenbaum, *I Love You, But I Don't Trust You: The Complete Guide to Restoring Trust in Your Relationship* (Berkley, 2012), 25.

CHAPTER 14: WHAT IS TRUST?

1. Henry Cloud, *Trust: Knowing When to Give It, When to Withhold It, How to Earn It, and How to Fix It When It Gets Broken in Life and Business* (Worthy, 2023), 33.

2. Cloud, *Trust*, 36-37.

CHAPTER 15: CAN I TRUST THEM AGAIN?

1. Lisa Wald, "The Science of Earthquakes," U.S. Geological Survey, https://www.usgs.gov/programs/earthquake-hazards/science-earthquakes.

2. Brad Hambrick, "Manipulative Repentance: 8 Red Flags Phrases," Brad Hambrick blog, January 20, 2017, https://bradhambrick.com/manipulative-repentance-8-red-flag-phrases/.

3. Tasha Eurich, *Insight: The Surprising Truth About How Others See Us, How We See Ourselves, and Why the Answers Matter More Than We Think* (Crown Currency, 2017), 18.

CHAPTER 16: CAN I TRUST ANYONE AGAIN?

1. Kobe Campbell, *Why Am I Like This?: How to Break Cycles, Heal from Trauma, and Restore Your Faith* (Thomas Nelson, 2023), 48.

2. Allen Ivey, Mary Bradford Ivey, and Carlos P. Zalaquett, *Intentional Interviewing and Counseling: Facilitating Client Development in a Multicultural Society* (Cengage Learning, 2018), 115.

3. Campbell, *Why Am I Like This*, 71.

4. Peter Scazzero, *Emotionally Healthy Spirituality: It's Impossible to Be Spiritually Mature, While Remaining Emotionally Immature* (Zondervan, 2017), 19.

CHAPTER 17: CAN I TRUST MYSELF AGAIN?

1. Lisa Wald, "The Science of Earthquakes," U.S. Geological Survey, https://www.usgs.gov/programs/earthquake-hazards/science-earthquakes.

2. Leslie Vernick, *The Emotionally Destructive Relationship: Seeing It, Stopping It, Surviving It* (Harvest House Publishers, 2007), 22.

CHAPTER 18: CAN I TRUST GOD AGAIN?

1. Dane Ortlund, *Gentle and Lowly: The Heart of Christ for Sinners and Sufferers* (Crossway, 2020), 151.

ACKNOWLEDGMENTS

Writing this book is by far one of the hardest things I've ever had to do. I think the only thing that's been harder is learning how to live out its principles. For this reason, I have many people to thank. First, I want to thank God! There were so many moments along this two-year journey when I wanted to give up. Thank You for making Your strength perfect in my weakness.

To my Momma, Ronion Henry: Thank you for always believing in what God could do through me, for getting me the reading and writing assistance I needed when the teachers pointed out I was struggling. None of this is possible apart from your love and faithful advocacy.

To my homies: Bree Carnes, Portia Purcell, and Cleo White, thank you for holding me down with your friendship and lifting me up in prayer throughout this process. Bree, you have been a friend that sticks close. Thank you for loving me when I'm wrong and in need of forgiveness. Thank you for enduring living with me during the process of writing this book, listening to almost every idea that came to my mind and making sure I didn't lose my mind in the process. Portia, thank you for calling out gifts in me I'm often too scared to see. This book is the fruit of your faithful encouragement. Cleo, thank you for always being willing to do the work of humbly admitting and confronting our sin together for the sake of maintaining the shalom in our friendship.

To Sandy Hafeez: Friend, what a gift it has been to do life together over these past 20 years. Thank you for your discipleship during my Dark Ages, your friendship during the highs and lows, and the gracious way in which you live with others. You have taught me so much about how to live as a shalom-maker in a broken world with fallen people.

To Omar and Latoya King: You two are some real ones. Not only are y'all the flyest couple I know, but you are also the wisest and most loving. Omar, thank you for being my brother and a thought partner. Toya, regular Wednesday morning coffee has been a gift. Thank you for every laugh, thoughtful question, and word of wisdom.

To Pastor Ryan, Lady A, and Vertical Church: I came to you wounded and not only did God use you to heal me, but to also bring about my thriving. Thank you for being my ride-till-we-die family. May we continue to love hard, laugh hard, and fight hard for one another to see others believe, belong, and become.

To Chris Pappalardo: Fam! God did it! Thank you for coaching me through this process. You made this book better. Thank you for every thoughtful edit and every encouraging word. I'm not sure if I would've finished without your accountability and support.

To Erik Wolgemuth, my book agent: Your support during this process has been invaluable. Thank you for advocating faithfully for me in this process.

To Audrey Greeson, acquisitions editor at Harvest House: Thank you for ignoring me when I tried to *not* write this book and your encouragement along the way.

To Lindsay Lewis, marketing manager at Harvest House: In so many ways, this book doesn't exist without you. Thank you for believing God had given me something to say and opening the door for this opportunity. And thank you, most importantly, for humbly confronting the ways I was still withholding forgiveness in my relationship with my dad and for your accountability to follow through when my resolve was wavering.

And finally, to the O.G. Elizabeth Woodson: You went from being one of those new friends I wasn't too sure about to being a true one. Thank you for being a source of encouragement and wisdom as I dared to write this book and for your thoughtful and skillfully written foreword. You a real one.

To learn more about Harvest House books and
to read sample chapters, visit our website:

www.HarvestHousePublishers.com

HARVEST HOUSE PUBLISHERS
EUGENE, OREGON